FORBIDDEN HISTORY

ANCIENT ECHOES

From Göbekli Tepe to the Antikythera Mechanism: The Proof That Advanced Civilizations Existed Long Before Recorded History

Ben Wilder

FORBIDDEN
HISTORY

Table of Contents

Introduction

The Proof Hidden in Plain Sight

What if we are not the first?

W hat if we are not the first advanced civilization on Earth, but merely the latest?

This question strikes at the foundation of everything we think we know about ourselves. For centuries, the prevailing story has been that civilization began in Mesopotamia around 4000 BCE, with the rise of city-states, writing, and organized religion. Yet scattered across the world are silent stone witnesses, mechanical wonders, and maps that should not exist. They are the whispers that suggest the story is incomplete.

Consider the hill country of southeastern Turkey. Beneath layers of soil lay Göbekli Tepe, a site older than agriculture itself. Its towering stone circles are carved with animals, celestial motifs, and symbols no one has yet decoded. Archaeology dates it to 9600 BCE, a time when humans were supposedly only hunter-gatherers. Yet its builders displayed architectural sophistication that should not have emerged for another five thousand years.

Or take the corroded bronze lump salvaged from a Mediterranean shipwreck, known as the Antikythera Mechanism. Beneath its crust, a set of gears interlocks with precision, tracking planetary cycles with an accuracy not matched again until the great clockmakers of the Renaissance. Made more than two thousand years ago, it is nothing less than a computer disguised as a relic.

And then there are the sky maps. Some carved on rock, others encoded in oral traditions, they suggest knowledge of constellations, precession, and star cycles far beyond what conventional history grants to early people. Why would hunter-gatherers track the wobble of Earth's axis across millennia? Unless they inherited knowledge from someone who had already studied the stars.

These are the ancient echoes: artifacts, monuments, and stories that should not exist, yet they do.

What are ancient echoes?

Ancient echoes are not fantasies. They are real fragments of stone, metal, and memory. They are the anomalies that sit uneasily within the puzzle of history. A figurine of a bird in Egypt, aerodynamic enough to resemble a glider. A map from the sixteenth century that seems to chart Antarctica's coastline free of ice. Megaliths so vast, like those at Baalbek in Lebanon, that even today, engineers debate how they could have been moved.

These echoes do not speak individually; they resonate together. Viewed collectively, they reveal a pattern too consistent to ignore: civilizations may have risen before us, mastering sciences, technologies, and cosmologies, only to vanish in catastrophe or to be erased by time. Their legacy survives not in continuous memory, but in fragments, scattered relics, oral traditions labeled as myth, and monuments standing like broken teeth in landscapes of silence.

Why do we not hear about them?

If such fragments exist, why are they not central to education? The reasons can be summarized in three forces:

1. **The Knowledge Filter:** Evidence that does not conform to accepted timelines is often dismissed as error or fraud. Institutions protect their paradigms the way fortresses guard their walls. To admit a single anomaly is to risk the collapse of the entire structure.

2. **Catastrophic Forgetting:** Earth itself is not a stable archive. Floods, earthquakes, comet impacts, and pole shifts erase entire

chapters of human history. What remains to us is not the whole story but fragments.

3. **Cultural Amnesia:** Myths are treated as stories for children, their great floods, cosmic battles, and sky gods dismissed as allegories. Yet what if myths are memories, distorted but rooted in real events, echoes preserved in the only way preliterate societies could manage?

The result is a paradox. The more extraordinary the artifact, the less likely it is to be accepted by conventional history. Our very system of knowledge discards the most crucial evidence.

You, the seeker

This book is not about indulging fantasy. It is an invitation to investigate the forgotten strata of human history. You, the reader, are not a passive observer. You are a seeker.

You are about to follow the trail of echoes left by forgotten civilizations: through stone, star, and silence. Some clues are carved into megaliths, others etched into ancient charts, and some built into machines that should not exist. Each clue opens a doorway into a different story of humanity.

This is not mythology, though myth will serve as a guide. This is not a conspiracy, though suppression of knowledge plays its part. This is evidence. Fragmentary, enigmatic, but evidence nonetheless.

The journey ahead

The path of this book is a journey into the shadows of prehistory:

- Part I will explore the technologies that seem to defy time: machines of impossible precision, metals of lost alloys, and the mystery of Göbekli Tepe.

- Part II will turn to the skies: ancient calendars, cosmic maps, and hints that humanity may have navigated oceans and stars long before it is credited with compasses or ships.

- Part III will examine catastrophe: sudden resets of human progress through fire, flood, and celestial impact, erasing civilizations and leaving only echoes behind.

- Part IV will confront the implications: if civilizations have risen and fallen before, what does that mean for us, the latest in line?

A companion workbook offers timelines of anomalies, celestial mapping exercises, and reflections to make the investigation interactive and personal.

Why this matters now

We live in an age where technology strips back the Earth's secrets. LIDAR has revealed forgotten cities beneath jungles. DNA studies have shown unexpected mingling between human species. Artificial intelligence uncovers structure in myths once thought random.

The echoes are being amplified by our modern tools. As we rediscover them, one truth becomes clear: humanity has risen before, and humanity has fallen before. Ignoring this pattern may condemn us to repeat it.

The ancients left us clues. Their voices echo through stone, metal, and sky. The question is not whether they existed, but whether we are finally ready to listen.

The Knowledge Filter

Archaeology often discards discoveries that do not fit existing timelines. When an excavation reveals an "impossible" artifact, such as a tool embedded in strata millions of years old, it is usually explained away as contamination. Yet this reflex may itself be the greatest barrier to rewriting history.

Part I: Technologies That Defy Time
Chapter 1: The Antikythera Mechanism

Picture a sponge diver kicking along the seafloor in clear Aegean water, seeing a glint inside a lump of coral and bronze, then tugging at something that looks like a barnacled plate. The crew hauls it up, it dries, and inside the crackled mineral crust, a set of interlocked bronze teeth appears. The find looks humble, it is fragmented and ugly, yet it carries a secret that should not exist where and when it was found. What sits in front of us is a mechanical mind cast in bronze, a machine that encodes the heavens into ratios, pointers, and inscriptions. If you hold it in your imagination and turn its crown by hand, the Sun advances, the Moon swells and thins with its variable speed, eclipses queue up along a spiral scale, and festival years click by. The device is real, not a legend, and that reality is the shock.

You and I are not here to marvel passively. We are here to understand how this instrument worked, why it was built, who might have needed it, and what its existence implies about the technological landscape that produced it. We will walk the mainstream path, then we will step off the paved road and examine the anomalies that do not fit neatly.

What is the mechanism in plain language?

Take a pocket calculator, remove the display and the batteries, replace the electronics with a forest of carefully cut gears, give those gears tooth counts that match astronomical cycles, attach pointers to dials that carry Greek inscriptions, mount everything inside a wooden case with hinged doors, then power it with a single hand crank. That is the essence. The mechanism translates turns of a handle into the changing positions of the Sun and Moon against the zodiac, the phase and varying speed of the Moon, and the long rhythms by which eclipses repeat. The back of the device tracks the repeating patterns of months and years on spiral scales, including cycles known to Greek astronomers that organize calendars, eclipses, and athletic games.

If this were built in the European fourteenth century, nobody would raise an eyebrow. Built in the second or first century before the common era, it changes the conversation about ancient capabilities. The calendar is not etched on stone here; it is computed. The heavens are not described in lines of text here; they are simulated in metal.

The device at a glance

Date: Hellenistic to early Roman period, roughly second to first century BCE.

Material: Bronze gear trains inside a wooden case with doors; Greek inscriptions on plates and around the dials.

Core functions: Solar and lunar position against the zodiac; lunar phase with variable speed; eclipse prediction using long cycles; long calendars for months and festival years; subsidiary cycles for fine corrections.

Use case: Education, demonstration, calendar regulation, eclipse prediction, and the display of astronomical knowledge in a compact instrument

Weathered bronze gearwork in a wooden box

From shipwreck to workshop in your mind

The device came from a wreck that held luxury cargo: fine statues, precious goods, and objects bound for elite buyers. A small, hand-cranked astronomical computer fits that cargo profile. You can imagine it being commissioned by a patron who wanted the cosmos made tactile, or ordered for a school where advanced students learned by demonstration, or carried by an astrologer who used eclipses and lunations to compose almanacs. The machine is not a toy; it is a learned instrument. It also appears to be a product of a mature shop culture. One artifact like this implies tooling, pattern gear blanks, practiced methods for cutting accurate teeth, and craftsmen familiar with astronomical specifications. A one-off object can be stunning; a one-off that works suggests a pipeline behind it.

Hellenistich Bronze-Gear Workshop
ca. 2nd-c. BCE (Antikythera-era)

A clockwork computer 2,000 years too advanced

Computation here is not electronic. It is a ratio and rotation embodied in metal. Each gear pair encodes a fraction. Multiply enough of those fractions in series, and you reproduce a complex astronomical cycle as a simple turn of a pointer. The builders laid out several trains of gears that branch and recombine to drive multiple dials at once. Some gears rotate on fixed posts; others ride on moving carriers, which lets the designers model irregular motions.

The front face is a story of the sky as seen from Earth. A large round dial bears the zodiac, the twelve equal sectors by which the ecliptic is measured. Another circular scale carries a calendar of days and months. One pointer represents the Sun across the zodiac, another the Moon. A small marker attached to the Moon pointer indicates its phase, so with a glance, you can see if the Moon in the sky will be thin or full. The subtlety goes further. The Moon does not move at a perfectly uniform rate relative to the stars. The machine captures that unequal motion by means of a clever compound arrangement that makes the Moon sometimes run a little faster, sometimes a little slower, in step with known theory.

Turn the device around, and you meet spiral dials. Imagine a flat spiral etched with month boxes, three or five turns from center to rim. A small slider rides along the spiral as the years pass. One spiral follows the pattern of months in a nineteen-year cycle that reconciles lunar months with solar years. Another spiral follows a longer period by which eclipses repeat. When the eclipse spiral tells you that the season is ripe, the device also shows you where in the zodiac those events are likely to occur.

Antikythera Mechanism- Front Dial

The cycles that live in the gears

Several cycles organize the dials. You do not need to memorize names to see the logic, yet the names reveal the depth of inherited knowledge. A nineteen-year cycle brings lunar months and solar years back into alignment. A longer cycle of a few hundred lunar months governs eclipse seasons and repeats. A multi-decade correction tightens accuracy by adding a small adjustment every so often. The device also includes a four-year register that lines up with the rhythm of major Greek games. This register is not frivolous. It ties the sky to civic timekeeping, festivals, and social life. Calendars anchor communities. Precision helps with festivals that are supposed to fall in particular seasons. When agriculture and religion are rhythm-based, the ability to keep months synchronized with the Sun becomes valuable.

If you think of the machine as a calculator, those cycles are its stored constants. Each constant lives as a gear ratio. When you turn the crank once for a day or a set interval, the device multiplies your input by those ratios mechanically. The output is a changing pointer position. A human composer of a table would have done the same multiplication on wax or papyrus. The machine reduces the chance of arithmetic error and makes the computation reversible. Set a pointer to an upcoming date, then read off what the sky will be doing.

The secret at the heart, variable motion cast into metal

The most striking intellectual feature is the treatment of the Moon's uneven speed. Ancient astronomers noticed that the Moon does not move across the stars at a constant daily rate. It slows and quickens in a pattern that repeats over a long interval. The device models this not with a table and a correction, but with a mechanical trick. One gear carries a pin that engages a slot in a companion wheel that is mounted on a moving carrier. As the carrier turns, the pin drives the slot in such a way that the output momentarily leads or lags the uniform input. The result is a graceful oscillation superimposed on the Moon's average motion. With that, the pointer for the Moon acquires the same kind of irregularity that the real Moon displays in the sky.

This is not just a craft skill. It is a theory embodied. The designers had to understand the abstract model that explains the Moon's anomaly, then translate that into tooth counts and offsets that a metalworker could realize. It is one thing to see that the Moon's motion is not constant. It is another to design a rotating carrier and a pin-and-slot pair that amplify or retard motion by the right amount at the right points in the cycle.

The inscriptions, a manual on metal

Around the dials and inside the covers, finely carved Greek text acts like labels, captions, and operating hints. The text lists cycles, gives month names, and remarks on phenomena. Think of it as a user interface engraved in bronze. The style of lettering suggests a learned audience, yet the instruction tone is practical. The whole device is a textbook you can turn with your hand. Where a scroll would present rows of numbers, this presents living pointers. Where a lecture would speak of cycles, this shows them moving. When you shut the doors, the inscriptions continue as dense panels of explanatory text. The case is an instrument and a book combined.

Greek Inscription on Hellenistic Bronze (Macro)

How it rewrites our understanding of ancient science

Now we address the phrase that made the device famous in popular discussion. Compared to the surviving record, nothing like this appears again for well over a thousand years. Medieval European clocks with trains of toothed wheels arrive far later, and those clocks often lack the mathematical subtlety that this ancient instrument displays. The gap between the Antikythera device and later geared astronomy suggests one of two possibilities. Either we have stumbled upon the peak of a lost tradition that mostly perished, or a small circle carried this knowledge forward quietly and intermittently, then it resurfaced in new contexts centuries later.

The conservative view says that the mechanism was the product of a few brilliant workshops in the Hellenistic world. The evidence is thin, not because the technology never existed elsewhere, but because bronze was precious and wooden cases rot away. Looting, recycling, and time erased most physical examples. Surviving texts do refer to geared spheres, model skies, and automata. Those references fit naturally with the existence of such a device. In this view, the mechanism is dramatic, yet it does not force us to imagine unknown continents of technology. It extends what we already knew the best Greek minds could do.

The heterodox view notices the density of skill required and the completeness with which it appears here. It points out that a single device of such refinement usually implies intermediate steps in a lineage. Where are those steps? It points to the tight tolerances, the variety of tooth counts, the design of carriers and axles, and the confident way theory is laid into metal. It asks if there were schools that trained mechanics to think this way, if there were manuals or house patterns that guided gear ratios, and if similar devices existed in wood for shorter-term use. It also asks why, if this existed, the tradition did not proliferate. Perhaps it did, then was erased by war, economic contraction, and the melting pot. Perhaps it survived in pockets, feeding later crafts through indirect channels.

How the workmanship reveals the shop culture

Study the teeth and you see regularity. Bronze gear teeth, cut and filed by hand, can still mesh smoothly if planning and jigging are good. Accurate tooth spacing likely came from a simple indexing method: scribe a circle, divide it by stepping with a pair of dividers set carefully from a master scale, file to the mark, test against a mating gear, then adjust. Holes for arbors are bored true and parallel. Plates are drilled and fitted so that stacks of gear can share space on the same axis without binding. The case carries bushings that reduce wear and keep things aligned. None of this happens by accident. It requires experience with backlash, with the need for slight clearance, and with the danger of cumulative error.

The mechanism also shows smart packaging. The designers balanced disk thickness, tooth height, and arbor placement to prevent interference. They used compound gears to compress long ratios into a compact footprint. They nested dials on the back in spirals to fit a

What counts as evidence of a tradition

Direct artifacts: additional mechanisms, tools, jigs, or partially finished gear blanks.
Indirect artifacts: inscriptions that list detailed gear counts or assembly steps, workshop inventories, or price lists for precision parts.
Textual witnesses: descriptions of planetariums, spheres, or calendars that include technical specifics, not just praise.
Transfer signals: later devices that show identical ratios or identical mechanical tricks, which implies copying from a common source.

long scale into a small circle. They respected the user by bringing all indicators to visible faces so you can read everything without disassembly. This is product design, not just theory.

What it could do for a working astronomer or calendar keeper

Imagine you are responsible for a city's lunisolar calendar. Farmers want months that keep pace with the seasons. Priests want festivals to land on the right phases. Sailors want to know when the Moon will be dark for night navigation or full for coastal travel. With the mechanism, you turn forward to the start of a civic year, set the pointers, then note the months where intercalation is appropriate. You identify eclipse seasons and warn that an eclipse is possible around certain dates. You plan festivals because the four-year cycle dial aligns with civic games. The value is not only in prediction. It is in coordination. When the mechanism says two cities will both see an eclipse season that year, messengers can carry that knowledge and align events. The instrument is a civic glue.

This has rhetorical power as well. A demonstration before the council, the students, or a patron is convincing. You can show the Moon's swelling and thinning as the days tick by under your fingers. You can mark a threatening eclipse season far in advance. Knowledge that previously lived as tables and rules becomes visible in a single motion.

Antikythera Lessons, c. 150 BCE – A reconstruction

The gaps that trouble tidy timelines

Now we face the hard question. If such an instrument existed in one port city, why do we not see cousins everywhere? Part of the answer is material loss. Bronze attracts smelters. Wood decays. Complex devices

How it rewrites the story of ancient science

Replaces static depiction with dynamic modeling: the heavens are computed, not only described. Bridges text and instrument: inscriptions act as a manual while the mechanism acts as a proof. Shows theory embodied: the lunar anomaly is not just a sentence, it is a mechanism. Suggests networks: such work implies communities of design, supply, and instruction.

are often broken into parts. Part of the answer is that our sample of the ancient world is thin. Even so, the silence is loud. The mechanism does not fit the stereotype of ancient technology as essentially simple machines and static monuments. It is a dynamic calculator in a portable box. It demands a revised mental portrait of the period, one where a minority of practitioners pushed technical thought into domains we had assumed were later inventions.

The phrase "two thousand years too advanced" captures the shock, but it can mislead. The device is not modern in its method. It is firmly ancient. It uses known cycles, not observational feedback. It is not a general computer. It is dedicated to a specific astronomical program. Its gears do not keep time by escapement; they merely transform input rotation into outputs. The conceptual advance is not that it discovered an unknown principle; it is that it integrated several known principles into a coherent, compact, and learnable machine. That integration is the marvel.

Mainstream, then heterodox, side by side

The mainstream account goes like this. Hellenistic science combined observation with geometry. Skilled mathematicians, working with instruments and tables, developed cycles that accurately reflect the motions of the Sun and Moon as seen from Earth. Artisans in cosmopolitan centers, exposed to high demand for teaching tools and prestige devices, learned to cast and finish bronze with precision. In that environment, someone conceived a hand-cranked demonstrator that could compress sophisticated astronomy into a box. The mechanism we have is a survivor from that culture. It is unique mainly because time ate its peers.

The heterodox account gives more weight to structure and silence. It asks whether the device's complexity implies a deeper tradition. It imagines a chain of prototypes, perhaps in cheaper materials like wood and leather, used for teaching and lost in damp libraries. It posits a network that drew from multiple sources, perhaps including earlier artisans from different regions of the Mediterranean and Near East, where gearwork and water clocks had long histories. It points to how quickly the design jumps to variable lunar motion with a compound carrier, and asks whether that leap was one mind's stroke or a shop's inherited move. It notes that the back dials integrate civic cycles with astronomical ones, which hints at repeated practical use in city administration, not only in a philosopher's school. In this view, the device is a late visible node of a mostly invisible web.

We can hold both views responsibly. The artifact proves capacity. It does not map the whole landscape. It tells us that at least one workshop could do this. It invites, rather than compels, the inference that more existed.

The mathematics inside, made tangible.

Consider what happens when you pick an astronomical cycle, say a certain number of lunar months, after which the pattern of eclipses repeats. You need an input shaft that represents days or months. You need a product that moves a pointer around a dial a certain number of turns in that time. If the cycle is 223 lunar months for an eclipse pattern, you must express that in a ratio of whole numbers that gear teeth can implement. Precision is achieved by selecting tooth counts that minimize error over the device's expected service life.

Ancient designers had a knack for selecting commensurable counts that keep tolerances under control. They also knew that a user reading a spiral dial is not measuring to seconds. The design targets the scale of the task. The eclipse indicator need not be perfect to the hour to be useful. It must flag seasons where eclipses are possible, and indicate roughly where in the zodiac they may occur. The Moon pointer, on the other hand, benefits from a pleasing match to the changing lunar phase. When the pointer shows a half Moon, the actual Moon near that date should look half-lit. The pin-and-slot solution achieves that aesthetic and practical goal.

Materials, fabrication, and tolerances

Bronze is chosen for a reason. It casts cleanly, it machines well with files and abrasives, and it resists corrosion better than pure iron. Thin plates can be shaped and drilled without cracking. Pins and arbors can be riveted or peened to hold stacks of wheels. The weak points are exactly where you would expect: thin gear teeth and pivots. Wear is managed by lubrication and by leaving slight play. Designers who understand that a rigid build binds will intentionally leave clearance so that dust or slight warps do not freeze the train. The wooden case is not decorative. It protects the mechanism from impact, dirt, and salt. Doors keep the inscriptions legible and the pointers safe.

The toolset is simple by modern standards. Hand files, bow drills, scribing compasses, dividers, abrasive stones, and simple lathes are enough. Precision is the product of patience and method. An indexing circle scratched from a master scale can produce tooth divisions that are remarkably even. A craftsman who tests a pair of wheels together, chalks high spots, and corrects with careful filing can get smooth action.

Comparing with later clockmaking without flattening the differences

It is tempting to see this as a medieval clock in a toga. That is not fair to either period. Later clocks introduced the escapement, a regulator that creates a steady tick and drives a time display without constant human motion. Our device has no such regulator. It relies on the operator's hand. Later, clocks expanded planet displays into elaborate astronomical clocks in town squares. Our device fits in a box and uses spiral scales. Later machines time the day, ring bells, and carry calendar complications. Our device aims at the heavens, not the hour.

The continuity is conceptual rather than mechanical. The idea that motion can be mathematically transformed with toothed wheels, that cycles can be embodied rather than merely written, that a pointer moving across a scale can teach better than a paragraph, these are points of resonance across centuries. When later clockmakers begin to add planetary indicators, they are moving toward what this device already did for the Sun and Moon.

What the instrument implies about education and institutions

An artifact like this survives only where several streams meet. There must be mathematicians who publish ratios. There must be artisans who can follow specifications and propose improvements. There must be patrons who appreciate the value, whether for prestige, instruction, or civic coordination. There must be audiences who understand what a demonstration means. In other words, there must be institutions that keep a shared language of theory and practice alive.

You can imagine a school that owns one such device. Senior students learned astronomy from a master who would set eclipses, then ask students to check tables against the pointer. A city could have borrowed the device for a calendar reform session. A wealthy traveler could have commissioned one to display erudition. Each of those use cases disciplines fabrication. The master complains if the pointer drifts. The city demands durability. The patron demands beauty. The shop responds by improving tooth form and engraving cleaner scales.

Stoa Lecture on a Hellenistic Astronomical Mechanism

The human factor, errors, and calibration

No mechanism is perfect. Wear shifts clearances, temperature swells wood and changes alignment, and gear teeth nick over decades of use.

The inscriptions act as a calibration guide. A user can set a known date and check the pointers. If the Moon pointer is off slightly, the user learns to interpret it with that offset in mind. This is the critical point. The device is not an idol of accuracy. It is a teaching and coordinating instrument that concentrates knowledge in a portable form. Its purpose is to connect cycles and to make them comprehensible in motion.

Calibration also keeps the community honest. If the device predicts an eclipse season for early spring in a certain zodiac sector, and one occurs near the predicted date, confidence rises. If a few pass without a visible event, the operator remembers that eclipses are not guaranteed at every season, only possible. The device teaches probabilistic thinking inside an ancient framework.

Why eclipses mattered

Eclipses are powerful social events. They terrify and fascinate. Being able to say, months in advance, that an eclipse season is coming grants authority. For sailors, a prediction that an eclipse season might occur during a voyage prepares minds for a day when the sky dims. For priests, the coordination of rituals around rare celestial events elevates the city's prestige. For scholars, a predicted eclipse that arrives near the forecast date is a vindication of method.

When you watch the eclipse spiral on the back dial advance with each crank, you see the power of long cycles. Human lives are short compared to the sky's slow recurrences. The device lets a single person carry centuries of patterns in their hands.

What would it take to build another one?

Suppose we strip the romance and ask a cold question. Could a Hellenistic shop reproduce this from scratch, given theory and demand? The answer appears to be yes. What is required is a specification book that lists cycles and tooth counts, a template for the case, and a set of tested tricks for variable motion. The bottleneck is not raw material or tools. It is coordination between theorists and makers, plus the time needed for an artisan to reach mastery.

In a world of trade networks across the Mediterranean, that coordination is plausible. Cities exchanged ideas along with goods. Scholars traveled for patronage. Artisans moved where demand existed. The device could be a high-end product within a niche market.

What we still do not know

Several mysteries remain open. We do not have the full build list with every original gear. Fragment loss leaves gaps. Scholars reconstruct plausible gear trains that fit the inscriptions, yet debates continue about exact tooth counts for some trains and the arrangement of certain indicators. We also lack an inventory of the shop's jigs and indexing plates. That limits our ability to judge production methods precisely.

There is also the larger historical question. Was this the crown of a small tradition that died out, or one branch of a broader tree whose wood and bronze simply did not survive? The responsible answer is humility. The device enlarges the space of the possible. It does not license fantasies. It presses us to look harder for texts that describe mechanisms with enough specificity that we can tie them to material practice.

How to read the mechanism as a human story

Beyond gears and cycles sits a human drama. Someone conceived the idea. Someone translated abstract cycles into tooth counts. Someone divided circles on bronze blanks. Someone stood at a bench and filed every tooth by hand. Someone checked the fit by ear, listening for smooth mesh. Someone composed the Greek captions, cut them into metal, and smiled when the letters caught the light. Someone closed the wooden doors, latched them, and loaded the instrument on a ship, proud of work well done. The mechanism is a team artifact, a witness to collaboration across specialties.

A fair reading of "advanced"

The word advanced often smuggles in a timeline. It suggests that technology must move in an orderly staircase, simple devices first, complex devices later. History is not that polite. Complex techniques can appear, flourish in a niche, then vanish. A fragile connection between theory and craft can snap when a workshop closes or a patron disappears. The mechanism is advanced not because it uses unknown physics, but because it integrates knowledge and craft with unusual completeness. It serves as an antidote to lazy narratives about gradual progress.

The right lesson is not that the ancients were secret moderns. It is that human ingenuity has deep roots, and that the conditions that support high craft are episodic. The mechanism is a high-craft event. It forces us to widen the variance of our mental model. If we once imagined a smooth slope from sundials to sandglasses to clocks to computers, we must now draw a rugged landscape with peaks separated by valleys.

Practical implications for the history of science

One artifact can recalibrate entire fields. Museum labels need to connect mathematics to metalwork. Histories of astronomy need to expand beyond observations and texts to include instruments that compute by motion. Courses on ancient technology need to highlight design thinking and user interface, not only labor and materials. The mechanism becomes a bridge topic. It connects calendrics, civic life, metallurgy, workshop practice, and the philosophy of modeling.

It also invites reverse engineering as a research method. Building replicas, whether physical or virtual, tests interpretations in a way that reading alone cannot. When a virtual model locks up, you know something is wrong with an assumed tooth count or clearance. When a physical replica binds because wood swells in humid air, you learn why a protective case and reasonable clearances are essential. The device turns historians into builders, and builders into historians.

How to think with the device today

Use it as a metaphor for translational thinking. Take a system of ideas and embody them in a medium that behaves. This is what good software does, what good policy does, and what good education does. The mechanism gives us a model of how to make abstract knowledge tangible without losing precision. It shows that a user interface can be engraved in metal and still teach clearly. It dignifies the craftsperson as a co-author of science.

It also reminds us that prediction can be participatory. A user turns the crank. The act of generating the future position of the Moon with your own hand creates a link between body and knowledge. Modern interfaces tend to hide computation. The mechanism reveals it. You see the train of cause and effect. You feel friction and clearance. You hear soft clicks as teeth mesh. The device teaches through all senses.

Questions worth taking away

Who funded the shops that made such instruments, and what did they want in return? How did mathematical theory circulate in a form that workshops could use? What other devices, now lost, paired with this one in an educated household? Which cities maintained calendars with help from such gearwork, and how did that shape civic identity? Did the tradition jump regions along trade routes? Did it influence, or get influenced by, water-clock makers, automaton designers, and navigators?

Each question is an opening for research. Each one acknowledges that the mechanism is not a final answer; it is a starting point that reframes our search image.

Field guide for future finds

Look for bronze plates with dense Greek text, even if fractured. Look for gear fragments with uniform tooth spacing and unusual thickness, not merely decorative wheels.
Look for wooden stains or mineralized voids in fittings that suggest a boxed case.
Look for ratios encoded in inscriptions that match known cycles. Document context carefully, since workshop debris can be as revealing as finished parts.

Closing perspective, a portable cosmos and a revised map of the ancient mind

Hold the device in your mind one last time. The front dial shows the Sun and Moon marching across the zodiac. The small phase marker waxes and wanes. The back spirals carry a long calendar through years and decades. A four-year register ties the sky to the civic heart. Everything is coherent. Everything is integrated. Each turn of the hand regenerates the cosmos in miniature.

We walk away with two convictions. First, this instrument demonstrates beyond debate that ancient technical culture could be integrative and precise at a very high level. Second, the survival of one such device means we must be cautious about grand statements based on sparse samples. A single surviving violin does not tell the whole story of a lost orchestra, yet it proves that the music existed.

To call the mechanism a clockwork computer two thousand years too advanced is to register our surprise. To see how it rewrites the narrative of ancient science is to respect what it actually did. It made the sky calculable to the hand and eye. It bridged theory and tool. It brought the abstract near. That is not an accident of genius. That is a society expressing its knowledge through craft.

Chapter 2

Sound, Stone, and Power

Y ou and I are going to listen first, then look. The oldest builders did not have loud engines or laser levels; they had stone, voice, drum, and corridors that carried a whisper like a wire. When we take sound seriously, the world's great stones stop being mute. They begin to perform.

The claim on the table

There are three pieces to examine. First, evidence that ancient monuments were tuned, not only aligned or decorated. Second, a practical question: can vibration help move or shape massive stones, and can we show a pathway from lab physics to fieldwork? Third, a case study that looks at "singing stones" in Peru and Egypt, asking what is solid, what is legend, and what tests we can repeat today.

We will move steadily, balancing mainstream archaeology, acoustical engineering, and the anomalies that keep researchers awake. You will see where the data is tight, where it is suggestive, and where it breaks open into possibilities that deserve field tests rather than slogans.

Evidence of acoustic technology in megalithic sites

Walk into a small stone room, speak a single low note, and feel the walls answer you. Many prehistoric chambers do this. The effects are not magical; they are measurable. Reverberation tails can be timed, resonant peaks can be plotted, and the way people respond to those acoustics can be studied with modern psychoacoustics. This is where the evidence is strongest.

Malta, Hal Saflieni Hypogeum: In a carved subterranean complex dating to the fourth millennium BCE, researchers documented strong resonances in the chamber commonly called the Oracle Room. Controlled tests reported peaks around 70 hertz and 114 hertz, within the vocal range of a baritone, and those notes launch sympathetic vibration through adjoining spaces. When a voice sits on those frequencies, the entire structure seems to "light up," and listeners report a sense that the sound is inside their bodies rather than only in the air. This is not folklore; it is a published acoustic finding.

Ireland, Newgrange, and other passage tombs: Field projects in archaeoacoustics have repeatedly found dominant resonances near 110 hertz in chambered sites, a band that couples well with human chanting. The details differ by site, but the pattern is notable: narrow stone spaces with curved or corbelled ceilings favor low frequencies that humans can easily sustain.

England, Stonehenge: When the circle stood nearer to completion, it was not only a sightline instrument. Acoustic engineers created a 1:12 physical scale model based on laser scans and archaeological reconstructions, then drove it with scaled test signals. The team found that the arrangement trapped and amplified sound created inside the circle, giving measurable reverberation and a sense of envelopment for instruments like drums and horns. The effect was not vast; it was focused, and it would have mattered to participants inside the ring more than to anyone outside it.

Peru, Chavín de Huántar: Here, the archaeology and acoustics come together with unusual clarity. The site yields both instruments, the marine conch trumpets known as pututus, and intact stone galleries with complex acoustic behavior. Experiments with original shells and with reconstructions show that the instruments can produce sustained tones and beat frequencies that travel through the labyrinth. Researchers have modeled source positions, measured how tones mask or disorient, and argued that sound was integral to ritual control, not a decorative extra.

These are not isolated curiosities. The pattern repeats: narrow, stone-lined volumes, curved or rounded internal geometry, and materials with high stiffness and low internal damping. Human voices and drums sit directly on the strongest modes. The experience is visceral. Even if we strip away any claims about "advanced lost civilizations," we still have engineering intent. Someone shaped space to shape the listener.

Hāl Saflieni Hypogeum – Oracle Room Acoustic Map
(Cross-Section)

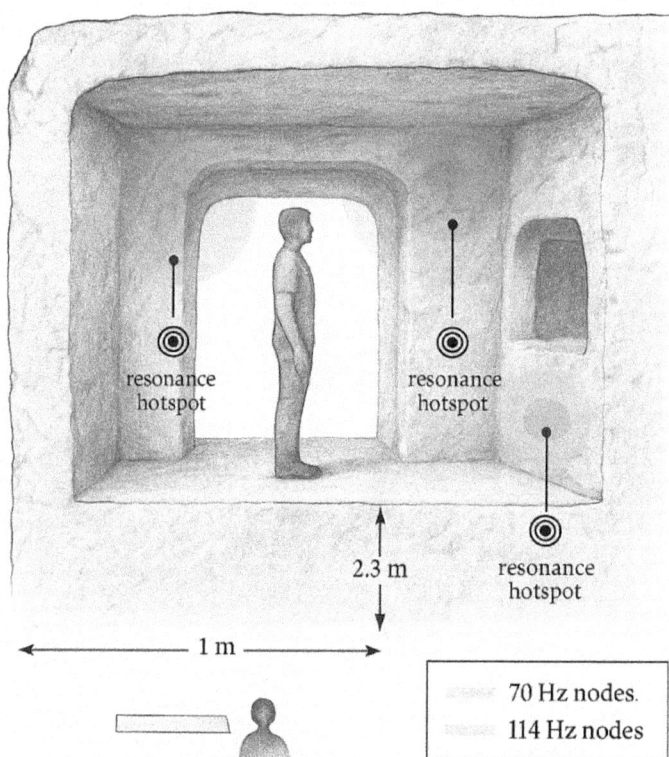

resonance hotspot

resonance hotspot

2.3 m

resonance hotspot

1 m

	70 Hz nodes.
	114 Hz nodes

Hotspot frequencies;
70 Hz & 114 Hz as reported by Debertolis et.
al.(2014–2015); broader peak at 72–76 Hz per Till, 2017
Antiqulty; positions approximate; see citations.

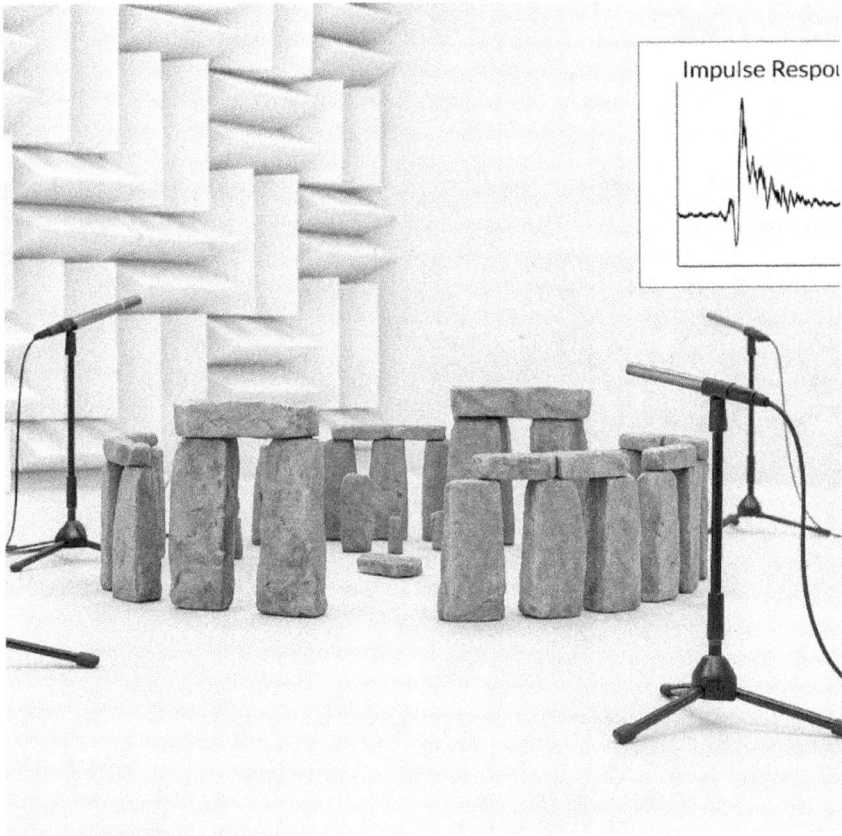

Measuring Stonehenge: 1:12 Scale Acoustic Test in an Anechoic Chamber

What acoustic design would have delivered, in practice

A tuned chamber changes three things: how intense a sound feels, how intelligible speech is, and how predictable the response is for a given performer. A baritone chant at the right pitch can feel "powered" by the room. Two players on shell horns can create beating patterns that make static tones feel like moving lights. In tight passages, a single drum hit turns into a rolling wave.

This matters in ritual. It sets a rhythm for coordinated action, it masks private speech near walls while amplifying public speech at a focal point, and it induces bodily sensations that communicate power without a word. You can call that theater, governance, or religion. In any case, it is technology.

Resonance is not volume, it is selectivity. A chamber that "likes" 110 hertz will ignore many other notes, but that one will bloom. When you see a site that rewards a particular vocal range, you are looking at a design constraint that could have guided who spoke, where they stood, and how a ceremony flowed. Focus on the coupling between voice pitch distributions in human populations and the favored modes of the space. Cite the Hypogeum 70 and 114 hertz findings as a template for fieldwork.

How vibrations may have moved or shaped massive stones

Here we must be careful and exact. There are three separate ideas that often get mixed together.

1. **Acoustic levitation:** In modern labs, ultrasound phased arrays can levitate and manipulate small objects. The physics is straightforward. Pressure gradients in a standing wave can create nodes that trap particles, and by shaping the phase of many emitters, engineers can move the traps and drag the particles with them. The best-known demonstrations lift beads and small bits of foam. This is real, repeatable, and published, but the forces drop fast with size. No one has levitated a megalith.

2. **Friction reduction by vibration:** granular materials, like sand under a sled runner, change character under vibration. Experiments and models show that small amplitude oscillations can weaken frictional contacts and induce transitions from stick-slip to sliding. In the language of geophysics, this is related to acoustic fluidization. At the scale of block hauling, the analogy would be a sled that is easier to pull when a team induces steady, low-frequency vibration. This is plausible physics, unlike full levitation, and it suggests concrete experiments at the human scale.

3. **Resonant shaping:** hammering at a stone with a rhythm that matches a small acoustic or elastic mode can change how energy flows into microcracks. Modern stonemasons already exploit thermal shock, water in wedges, or percussion rhythms to guide fractures. Could elite ancient teams have used rhythmic percussion, perhaps aided by sonorous markers, to speed pecking and dressing? Physics does not require mystery, only skill and time.

Let us separate the spectacular from the practical. Acoustic levitation is not a pathway to floating a hundred-ton block up a causeway; the field strengths and wavelengths do not scale kindly. Friction reduction by vibration is different; it is already used in industry, and it maps to ancient toolkits. The most promising historical mechanism looks like this: runners or sled bottoms on a prepared granular track, constant lubrication with water or clay slip, and percussion or chanting to maintain a steady team cadence while the track is excited by rhythmic impacts. The vibration weakens the "jammed" state of grains, the runner sees lower resistance, and the same human power pulls more mass per step. This is testable.

How to translate lab physics into a field protocol

A team could run a weekend experiment with rented blocks and a safe test ground.

1. Prepare two parallel tracks: dry sand on one, wetted sand with fine clay on the other.

2. Mount a vibration source that a human crew can control, for example, springy thumper boards or sledge impacts timed by a drum.

3. Instrument the pull line and the sled with load cells and accelerometers.

4. Run pairs of trials: silent pull versus metered impacts at 1 to 4 hertz, and measure average pull force over distance.

5. Repeat enough times to reach statistical confidence.

If the force drops in the excited condition, you have a direct bridge from geophysics to engineering practice. If it does not, you have ruled out one popular claim and can focus on slope, lubrication, and simple logistics.

Acoustic levitation shows that sound can move matter, but only at small scales with high intensities. Friction weakening under vibration is the scalable idea. Emphasize that this does not prove that any ancient culture used it, it only shows a credible mechanism that teams could apply with drums, thumpers, and cadence. Cite contemporary ultrasonic "tractor beam" research to explain why levitation does not scale to megaliths.

Case study: the "singing stones" of Peru and Egypt

The phrase "singing stones" covers two different phenomena. One is literal, rocks that ring when struck. The other is architectural, structures that sing when excited by voice or instrument. Peru and Egypt give us both.

Egypt: the Colossi of Memnon and the voice at dawn

On the west bank of the Nile near Luxor stand the seated quartzite colossi that once fronted the mortuary temple of Amenhotep III. Ancient visitors reported that at dawn, one statue "sang." Greek and Roman writers described a high, bell-like tone or a whistle. The phenomenon ceased after repairs in Roman times, which suggests a physical cause rather than pure myth. The best modern explanation is that dew and morning heat entered fine fissures in the stone, and as the temperature rose, the expansion and evaporation drove small vibrations that produced audible sound. The physics is akin to a kettling kettle; the theatrics were perfect for an oracle. The story reminds us that stone can be an instrument, sometimes by accident, sometimes by design.

Peru: when stone and sound work together

Peru gives us two tracks, and we should keep them separate so that each stands on its own evidence.

Track one, instruments and tuned spaces, Chavín de Huántar: Excavations recovered a cache of twenty marine conch trumpets, the pututus, at a temple with narrow stone galleries and ramps. Acoustic and psychoacoustic studies with original instruments, replicas, and the actual galleries show that the shells produce deep, steady tones and beating effects that travel and transform inside the architecture. The galleries' mask direction and confuse listeners, which would have been powerful in a ritual where the sound seems to come from the stone itself. This is the strongest Peruvian case for designed sound.

Track two, ringing or "singing" stones as objects: Lithophones are known worldwide, from Africa to India to China, and the basic principle is simple. Some rocks ring when struck, especially dense, elastic stones shaped to favor long ring times. Evidence within the central Andes for formal lithophone ensembles is scattered and often modern, while informal reports of ringing boulders exist throughout highland travelogues. There are localized Andean traditions of sonorous stone and of pillars or blocks that produce tones when tapped, but the best documented Peruvian "singing" is architectural, not object-based, and centers on Chavín's instrument-architecture duet. As we build the book, we should use Chavín as the Peruvian anchor, and we should treat solitary "ringing rock" anecdotes as prompts for field tests, not as finished facts.

Peru's hard data on singing stone comes from Chavín, where instruments and architecture were found together and studied together. Use Memnon to show that stones can sing by accident, then argue that Chavín shows how stone can be made to sing by design. Invite new fieldwork on Andean lithophones, but keep the claims restrained until there are instrument-grade measurements.

Chavín de Huántar Acoustics:
Pututu & Gallery Sound Paths

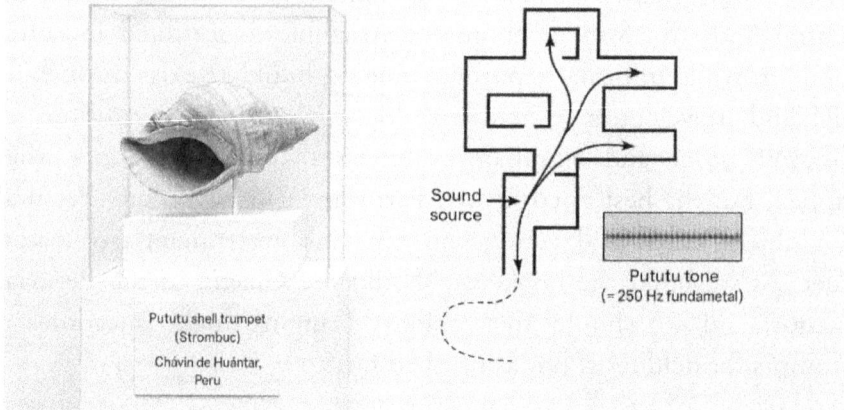

Sound source

Pututu tone
(= 250 Hz fundametal)

Pututu shell trumpet
(Strombuc)

Chávin de Huántar,
Peru

What counts as "technology," and what counts as "advanced"

A tuned room that can turn a single human voice into a building-filling instrument is technology. So is a calendar carved into light and shadow. If we define "advanced" as "able to control prior forces with precision and repeatability," then prehistoric acoustic design qualifies. The control here is not microelectronics; it is geometry, material choice, and human physiology. A chamber that blooms at 110 hertz privileges certain voices and instruments, carries sound down specific corridors, and may conceal speech at targeted spots while amplifying it at others. That is social engineering encoded in stone.

Mainstream archaeology is comfortable with this when the claims stay within physics and people. Where pushback starts is when someone jumps from "this room is tuned" to "they used ultrasound arrays to levitate granite." The first is measured; the second is a slogan that ignores scaling laws. We do not need to overclaim. The evidence is gripping on its own terms.

Building a test-ready research agenda from the anomalies

If you want this chapter to not only intrigue but also instruct, we need to translate the story into protocols that a field team could run without exotic gear. Four directions stand out.

A. Resonance mapping, fast and repeatable

Carry a compact loudspeaker and a calibrated microphone. Sweep from 60 to 300 hertz and record at a grid of points. Log decay times and peak frequencies. Publish the raw data, not only smoothed graphs, so other teams can reanalyze. This has already been done at several sites, and the method is robust. Use Hypogeum-style protocols as baseline.

B. Human response under controlled tones

Use safe sound pressure levels. Place volunteers in tuned spaces, play sustained low notes, and record subjective reports plus simple physiological markers, for example, breathing rate and skin conductance. Do not overinterpret, just correlate peaks in response with measured room modes.

C. Logistics tests for friction weakening

As outlined above, build tracks, pull sleds, and measure. If the force drop is real under rhythmic excitation, then we have a plausible tool to add to other known methods, such as water lubrication and rollers.

D. Artifact-architecture coupling in Peru

At Chavín, continue the integrative approach that treats instruments and corridors as a single design. Use pututu replicas that match the measured spectra of originals, then map where certain tones cause direction masking. Extend to other Andean sites where galleries and ramps could support similar effects.

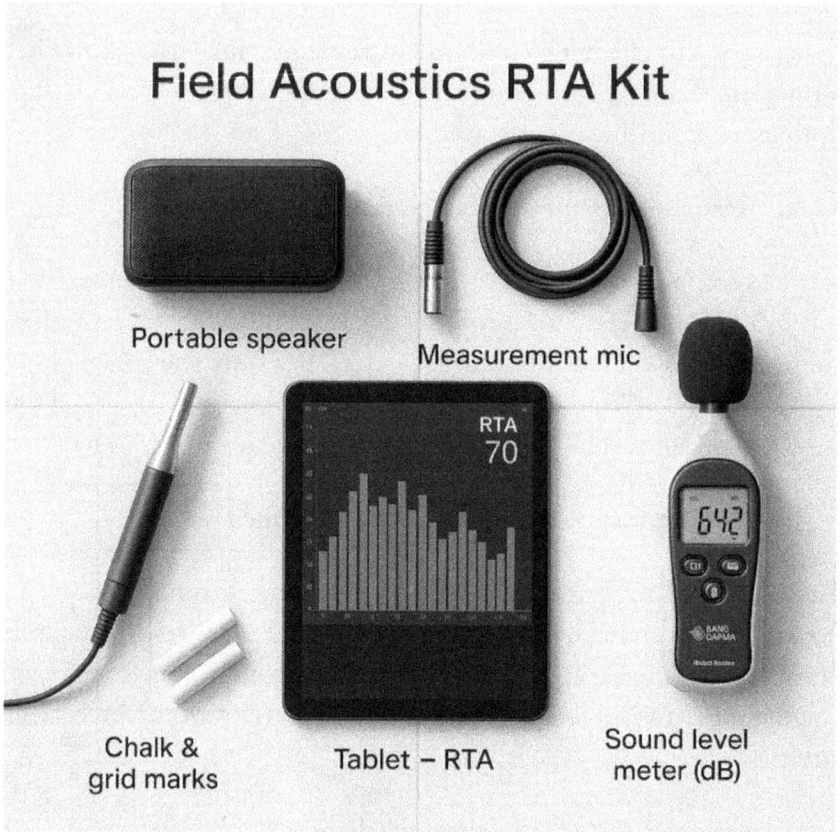

Field Acoustics RTA Kit

Portable speaker

Measurement mic

Chalk & grid marks

Tablet – RTA

Sound level meter (dB)

A guided listening tour through key sites

Take a step-by-step path. Imagine we are on-site with a small team.

Malta, Hal Saflieni Hypogeum

You enter the Oracle Room. One person stands at the niche that prior teams identified as optimal, another waits in the adjacent chamber. The speaker sustains a low A near 110 hertz, then moves to 114, then to 70. You log where the walls seem to "speak back." The data matches published peaks, which anchors your experience in repeatable numbers.

Ireland, passage tomb tradition

Short, low, stone-lined passages that flare into corbelled vaults favor very specific modes. A hum becomes a body-felt vibration. You realize that in a world without amplification, such a room gives a ritual leader an acoustic switch: one voice, many bodies, one frequency, shared sensation.

England, Stonehenge interior

The scale model results tell you that when the circle was more complete, sounds inside the ring were more coherent and enveloping than sounds outside. A drummer in the center could set a common pulse for a large group. The circle was not a concert hall; it was a close space carved from open air.

Peru, Chavín galleries

Instruments and stone work together. A pututu blast is not pretty like a modern horn; it is powerful and strange. In the dark, with limited sightlines, the mind assigns agency to the stone. Authority speaks without a visible mouth. This is how sound becomes governance.

Egypt, the Memnon dawn voice

You stand at sunrise and imagine the ancient tone. Whether it was a whistle from a tiny fissure or a more complex vibration, the fact that repair silenced it is the clincher. Nature can make an instrument by accident, and builders can do it on purpose.

Counterarguments and how to answer them without hype

"Resonance happens everywhere; it proves nothing about intent." Answer: Random rooms have resonances, that is true. Repeated selection for the same human-friendly bands, in spaces with shapes that amplify their effects, points to design. When you find an entire complex where measured modes match the known capabilities of local instruments and human voices, intent becomes the simplest explanation. Use Chavín as the model, because instruments and architecture are co-present.

"Singing stones are tourist myths."

Answer: Sometimes yes, sometimes no. The Memnon phenomenon is documented by ancient writers and explained in modern physical terms, and the fact that repairs ended it helps the case. Treat other claims skeptically until measured, and encourage careful in situ testing.

"Sound cannot move megaliths."

Answer: agreed for levitation, rejected for friction weakening without a test. Lab work shows that vibration reduces granular friction, which is relevant to sled and track logistics. Build experiments at the human scale before you make claims for or against ancient use.

Stand in a stone room with a friend. Ask them to hum slowly until the walls answer. Mark that note. That is the site's signature. Ask them to step two paces and do it again. Map the hot spots. You have just used your body as a spectrum analyzer, the oldest instrument of all. Now imagine a leader who knows that map by heart.

One sentence to remember

Sound is the oldest lever, stone is the oldest memory, and together they can move crowds more reliably than any forgotten machine.

Chapter 3

Lost Materials and Forgotten Alloys

If you sift through the rubble of an old harbor outside Naples, chip a small sample from a Roman breakwater, and peer at it under a microscope, something curious appears. The material looks less like modern cement and more like a living geology lesson, crystals threading through volcanic ash, seawater locked into mineral lattices, pores bridged by new growth that seems to heal tiny cracks over time. Pick up a blade with a rippling surface from a museum case, and, under the right light, the steel seems to have a watermark that is not painted or etched; it is grown from the metal itself during careful heating and cooling. Step beside the iron column in Delhi that has shrugged off centuries of monsoon seasons with only a faint chocolate patina, and the obvious question presents itself. Did people of the past know something we forgot, or are we projecting mysteries onto their craft because their notebooks did not survive, and their best shops did not scale into factories?

This chapter looks squarely at three famous cases. Roman concrete at the shore, Damascus steel with its deceptive pattern that is anything but cosmetic, and the so-called orichalcum that straddles myth and money. We will close with a focused case study on the Delhi iron pillar and what it teaches about process control without thermocouples, compositional windows without spreadsheets, and the power of tacit knowledge. Throughout, I will show you the mainstream explanations, then the places where anomalies remain, so you can judge how strong each claim is.

Roman concrete, Damascus steel, and mysterious "orichalcum"

Roman concrete: the stone that likes to get wet

Modern Portland cement is the backbone of cities. It sets quickly, it can be produced with uniform properties at an industrial scale, and engineers know how it behaves. Roman maritime concrete is something different. It was not a single recipe; it was a family of practices tuned by local ingredients. The usual constituents were quicklime, water, volcanic ash rich in reactive silica and alumina, and aggregate. The famous ash came from volcanic districts around the Bay of Naples, and similar materials exist elsewhere along the Mediterranean. When that ash met lime and seawater in a compact mass, minerals formed inside the hardened matrix that are rare in ordinary modern concretes used in marine settings. Those minerals fill and bridge pores, reduce permeability, and can slow down crack growth. The result is a concrete that matures for decades and even centuries, rather than becoming weaker with age.

Engineers today can reproduce the chemistry on paper, yet two practical hurdles remain. First, the microstructure forms in response to exact ash composition, moisture content, and temperature history, which vary from place to place. Second, the Romans often packed their mixtures with large stones and compacted them in tight forms, especially in cofferdams built in shallow water, so the geometry of pores and the way seawater circulated during curing mattered. This is the heart of the mystery. The ingredients are understandable, the process window is wide on paper, yet the path to the most durable microstructure seems to be narrow in practice.

Modern experiments with volcanic pozzolans and lime can indeed generate the same families of minerals found in ancient cores. Some mixes even show self-sealing of microcracks when water percolates through them. The challenge is repeatability at scale. A quarry face changes across meters, a kiln temperature drifts, an on-site crew alters compaction rhythm, then the long game of seawater contact begins. Reproducing the final performance requires tuning all these moving parts together.

Mainstream view: Roman maritime concrete is a lime-pozzolan system that benefits from ash chemistry and long-term interaction with seawater. Its resilience is not magic; it is a synergy among reactive volcanic glass, free lime, and marine ions that slowly build protective crystals and binders inside the matrix. The Romans did not reject all modern ideas; they prioritized durability over speed. Their material wins in environments where slow mineral growth benefits the structure, like seawalls and piers.

Heterodox view: Some argue that certain outlier samples show unusual crystal abundance or morphology that indicates a special additive, perhaps organic extracts or kiln procedures that modern reconstructions have not captured. Others contend that ancient builders practiced "hot-mixing," adding quicklime directly rather than fully slaking it first, which creates lime-rich clasts that later act as healing reservoirs. The debate is not whether such clasts exist; they do in some samples. The debate is how central that technique was across sites and whether it is the master switch for longevity.

Practical implication for today: if you are building a harbor where service life matters more than speed of turnover, a lime-pozzolan design with calibrated ash, coarse aggregate packing, and controlled moisture can outperform standard mixes over decades. The cost is slower early strength and the need to thoroughly qualify local ash.

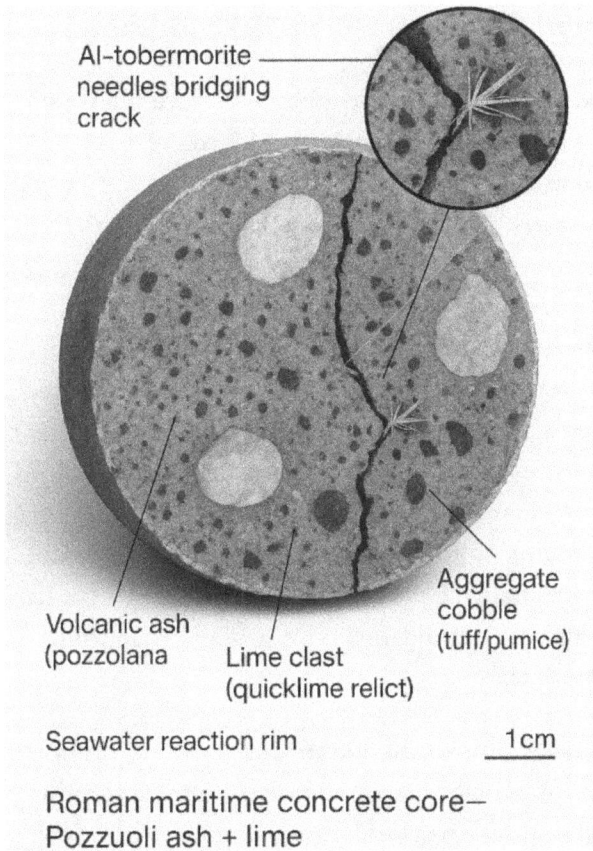

Al-tobermorite needles bridging crack

Volcanic ash (pozzolana

Lime clast (quicklime relict)

Aggregate cobble (tuff/pumice)

Seawater reaction rim   1 cm

Roman maritime concrete core—
Pozzuoli ash + lime

What actually sets Roman harbor concrete apart
- Volcanic ash rich in reactive glass, selected from specific districts.
- Lime and seawater environment that promotes slow crystal growth inside the hardened mass.
- Large aggregate blocks packed tightly, which reduce overall porosity and stabilize flow paths.
- Acceptance of slow early strength, patience that allows the microstructure to mature.

Damascus steel: a pattern that tells a thermal story

Say "Damascus steel" and many people picture the watered pattern on modern knives. Much of what is sold today uses pattern-welding, which is the art of stacking, twisting, and forging layers of different steels to create visible waves. That is a beautiful craft, and it can yield strong blades when done well, but it is not the historical Damascus that sparked centuries of fascination. The older tradition drew from crucible steels, sometimes called wootz in South Asia, made by melting iron with carbon and trace elements in sealed vessels, then cooling very slowly. When the resulting ingot was forged by a patient smith who kept temperatures in a specific band, carbide structures precipitated in lamellae and islands. Those carbides, along with banding from segregation during solidification, created both the visible pattern and part of the mechanical profile: edges that could be hard and wear resistant, spines that could flex, and a blade that could be sharpened keenly and hold it.

Mainstream view: historical Damascus patterns originated from the combination of crucible steel chemistry and a training system that taught smiths how to work those ingots without dissolving the carbides. If the metal was overheated, the fine structures dissolved and the pattern washed out. If the metal was worked too cold, it cracked. The supply chain mattered as much as the hammer. Specific ores containing trace elements like vanadium or tungsten, along with charcoal of certain qualities and crucible materials, set the stage for consistent carbide nucleation.

Why it is hard to replicate exactly: modern metallurgy can hit target carbon levels and add trace elements deliberately, and modern forges can control temperatures precisely. Even so, producing the exact historical pattern with the same distribution and size of carbides is nontrivial. Subtle variations in cooling rate through the eutectoid neighborhood, the number and timing of thermal cycles during forging, and the presence of specific impurities all change the result.

Several modern researchers have reproduced blades that look and cut like historical examples, but the craft is not plug-and-play. When you change the ore source or charcoal chemistry, you may need to retune the entire thermal schedule.

Heterodox view: a set of claims has circulated that historical Damascus contains exotic nanostructures that modern metallurgists cannot emulate, sometimes linked to assertions about catalytic growth of carbon nanotubes. The extraordinary claim is that these structures are the source of legendary cutting feats. The balance of evidence suggests that steel carbides, cementite networks, and impurity-assisted nucleation explain the visible pattern and the mechanical properties. The blades were very good because smiths controlled a narrow process window that aligned with their materials supply, not because of a mysterious extra ingredient that vanishes under examination.

A caution about names: a thousand modern "Damascus" blades are pattern-welded, which can be excellent steels, yet they are not the same metallurgical route as wootz-derived blades. Confusing the two muddies both craft histories. The takeaway is simple. The watered pattern can come from a layered assembly or from solid-state development within a crucible steel. The photograph alone cannot tell you the route with certainty, but etching response and microstructure can.

TWO STEELS CALLED "DAMASCUS":

PATTERN-WELDED VS CRUCIBLE (WOOTZ) – MICROSTRUCTURE CROSS-SECTIONS

Pattern-welded
(laminated)

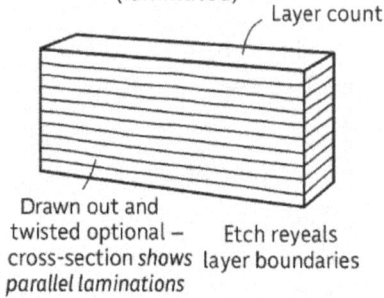

Layer count

Drawn out and
twisted optional –   Etch reyeals
cross-section *shows* layer boundaries
parallel laminations

| PATTERN-WELDED: |
| Etch reveals layers from |
| *N* alternating steels |

Crucible Damascus (wootz)

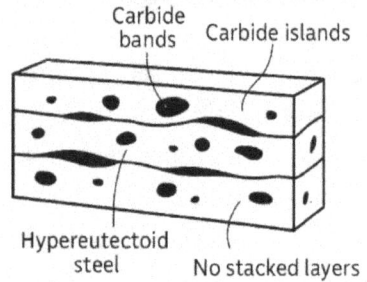

Carbide
bands   Carbide islands

Hypereutectoid
steel   No stacked layers

| CRUCIBLE DAMASCUS: |
| Etch reveals carbides |
| in single steel matrix |

How to read a Damascus pattern like a metallurgist

- Ask about the route: layered assembly or crucible origin.
- Look for carbide networks under magnification, not just cosmetic contrast.
- Examine etch behavior: carbide-rich areas resist etch differently than ferrite-pearlite.
- Mechanical feel matters: edge retention and toughness in real cutting tests.

Orichalcum: from Plato's gleam to a Roman mint

Orichalcum arrives in two very different contexts. In a Greek dialogue, it is a shining substance that decorates an idealized city. In Roman texts and coinage, it shows up as a practical alloy with a greenish-gold look, often used for high-status objects and coins. The simplest resolution of the confusion is linguistic. In later Mediterranean use, orichalcum referred to a copper alloy with a good dose of zinc, which we would today call brass. Romans did not have electrolytic zinc metal in bulk; instead, they made brass by heating copper with zinc-bearing minerals like calamine in sealed vessels. Zinc vapor diffused into the copper, raising the zinc content to a brass composition. The product could be quite bright and stable, and it resisted tarnish better than pure copper. When you strike coins or cast fittings from such an alloy, you get the golden appearance of orichalcum without a single fleck of precious metal.

Mainstream view: orichalcum in practice is brass made by cementation, tuned by experience. The process is very sensitive to temperature and atmosphere, since zinc boils off if heating runs too hot or too long, and the mineral charge varies from mine to mine. Experienced foundries could hit a repeatable range and select for color and workability. Archaeological finds of ingots that test as brass fit this picture well.

Heterodox view: since Plato's account associates orichalcum with a lost island and heroic architecture, some writers propose that the term originally meant an exotic alloy with special properties that later cultures could not reproduce, so they attached the name to something more ordinary. That possibility is hard to test, since the dialogue is not a technical manual and does not include recipes. The most economical reading is that the glow of myth fused with the glow of a common yet elegant alloy, which, in the right light, can look like a cousin of gold.

The lesson here is about names and memory. A single word can point to two different things: a metaphor in one era, a mint master's product in another. When we ask whether a material is "lost," we should first ask whether the vocabulary has drifted. In this case, one strand of the story is philosophy and allegory, the other is furnace practice with zinc minerals and copper.

Materials modern science struggles to replicate.

It is tempting to say that modern science can recreate anything if given enough time and budget. In principle, that is often true. In practice, exact replication fails for reasons that have nothing to do with equations and everything to do with context.

First, feedstocks were specific. The ash that Romans favored came from particular volcanic glasses with particular minor elements. The iron ores that fed crucible steel traditions could supply traces that mattered for carbide behavior. The zinc minerals used for brass varied in purity and volatiles. You can match the main elements easily, yet still miss the trace fingerprints that steer microstructures during slow transformations.

Second, the process history was slower and more tolerant of time. Many ancient shops valued a long cure, a slow cool, a season of weathering. That long tail creates phases that do not appear in accelerated lab schedules. Patience is a process parameter. It is hard to sell patience on a project timeline, yet materials like Roman maritime concrete grow into their strength because water keeps working the matrix for years.

Third, tacit knowledge filled the gaps that modern engineers would assign to sensors. The crucible worker could smell the charcoal and read the glow, the lime burner could hear the crackle that marks the right stage of slaking, and the mason could feel the right bounce under the rammer. Those skills do not leave a neat algorithm behind. When the line of apprenticeship breaks, you can recover the steps but not the instincts without long practice.

Fourth, the target performance in antiquity was not identical to ours. Romans would accept slow strength in exchange for durability in salt water. A sword culture would accept a higher scrap rate if the surviving blades were superb. A mint might focus on color and corrosion resistance rather than maximizing conductivity. Modern priorities push toward speed, uniformity, and global interchangeability.

With these four in mind, the fact that we can, in controlled projects, reproduce the main features of Roman concrete, crucible Damascus, and calamine brass is a testament to how much we understand. The fact that we still struggle to deliver those features cheaply, consistently, and at scale is not a failure of science; it is a reminder that the supply chain and the shop floor are part of the material.

Case Study: The Iron Pillar of Delhi, a metal that refuses to rust

The Delhi iron pillar stands in the open air, over seven meters tall, a monument from late classical India that has endured an environment that would eat most bare steels alive. Visitors notice the surface color, a deep brown that looks more like leather than rust. The inscription credits a ruler and a religious dedication, yet the metallurgical marvel is the body of the pillar itself: forged from large pieces of wrought iron, joined and hammered into a coherent column that has resisted serious corrosion for well over a millennium.

What is wrought iron, and why does it matter here? Before mass steelmaking, ironworkers reduced ore in furnaces that did not fully melt the iron. The product was a spongy bloom with entrained slag, which was reheated and hammered to squeeze out liquid slag and weld the iron together. The resulting material, wrought iron, is nearly pure iron with strings of slag particles aligned by working. Those slag inclusions are not a defect in this case; they are part of the corrosion story.

The pillar's corrosion resistance is not a blanket miracle. It is the outcome of composition, microstructure, environment, and time. The iron has relatively high phosphorus by modern standards, because furnaces and fluxes of the day did not remove it efficiently. The slag strings distribute the phosphorus unevenly near the surface. In the humid and often mildly acidic environment of Delhi's climate, the surface reacted to form a thin protective layer enriched in iron oxyhydroxides and phosphate compounds. That layer is adherent and relatively insoluble; over time, it thickens slowly and seals pores. When the layer remains intact, oxygen and moisture penetration slow dramatically, and the underlying iron is protected.

Mainstream view: the pillar resists corrosion because its wrought iron contains enough phosphorus and retains slag structures that help form a passive film under local conditions. The builders' skill in forging a large, mostly defect-free column ensured that the protective film could remain continuous over large areas. Where mechanical damage or pollutants attack the surface, rust can occur, and some patches show ordinary corrosion behavior. The pillar is not immune to rust; it is unusually good at forming a self-limiting patina.

Heterodox view: popular accounts sometimes claim that the pillar is meteoritic iron, or that it contains secret alloying ingredients unknown to modern metallurgists. Those claims do not align with the observed microstructure of wrought iron or with the presence of slag stringers typical of bloomery products. Another claim is that the pillar proves ancient people could produce stainless steel. That overstates the case. The pillar is a showcase of how specific impurities and process routes can produce long-term stability without chromium or modern passivation, not an early stainless alloy.

What was hard about making it? The scale alone is impressive; welding and consolidating large blooms into a straight, tall pillar without trapped voids takes meticulous reheating and hammering. The workers did not calculate diffusion rates on paper; they iterated techniques until the welds were sound and the section was uniform. The result is a column with enough cohesion to avoid cracking as it cooled and enough integrity that the protective film could do its job.

What it teaches today. First, small compositional differences can have big surface effects after decades of exposure. Second, slag is not always a vice; in this context, it is part of the cure. Third, passive films can work without the elements that modern stainless steels rely on, provided the environment helps and the microstructure cooperates. Fourth, a monument can remain an experiment that is still running, a data point for long-term corrosion in real air and real rain.

Field notes for corrosion geeks at the pillar

- Look for color variation to spot different film thickness.
- Examine any repairs or scratches to see fresh metal vs passivated metal.
- Note nearby pollutants or bird activity, which can localize corrosion.
- Observe drainage paths at the base, since water retention changes behavior.

Roman concrete, Damascus steel, and orichalcum, what they share

At first glance, these three topics live in separate worlds. One is masonry that grows stronger in seawater, one is a blade that carries a pattern in its very microstructure, and one is an alloy name that straddles myth and mint practice. Their shared core is process sensitivity.

Roman maritime concrete requires the right ash and the right patience. Damascus, in the crucible tradition, requires the right trace elements and strict thermal discipline. Orichalcum requires careful control of a vapor-phase alloying route that punishes excessive heat. In every case, the recipe written as a list of ingredients is not enough. The method section matters as much as the materials section.

This is why "modern science struggles to replicate" can be true even when the thermodynamics are straightforward. It is not about a missing element on the periodic table; it is about dialing in a many-variable process such that the final microstructure lands in a sweet spot. Engineers can hit that spot in a lab, yet keeping it there when feedstocks vary and crews rotate is much harder.

There is also a social dimension. Historically, knowledge lived in guilds and workshops. A master might share many steps with an apprentice, but a few subtle signals might only transfer after years of standing at the fire together. If the chain of custody breaks, the next generation must rediscover those signals. Written treatises mention temperatures by color and timing by the pace of a chant. That is enough for someone already inside the craft, not enough for a stranger to start from zero.

Testing the boundaries: what counts as "advanced"

This book argues that human cultures, long before our modern industrial era, sometimes achieved performances that look advanced even by today's standards. In materials, the trap is to define "advanced" by brand-new compositions alone. A better standard is to ask whether a material meets a demanding brief in a way that is hard to reproduce without the original context.

By that standard, Roman maritime concrete is advanced because it thrives in a chloride-rich environment that destroys many modern concretes unless they use specialized binders and admixtures. Crucible Damascus is advanced because it couples esthetics with a mechanical profile that depends on steering carbides at micrometer scales using only the eye, hammer, and heat. Orichalcum is less about extraordinary performance than about the ingenuity of process, since making a zinc-containing alloy before you can purchase zinc metal demonstrates a deep understanding of furnace atmospheres and volatility. The Delhi pillar is advanced not for corrosion immunity in any environment but for passive stability in a real climate over long times without modern alloying.

The key qualifier is this: advanced relative to context. If you replace local ash with a synthetic blend and shorten curing using accelerators, you have changed the system. If you add chromium to make stainless wrought iron, you have changed the question. The fascination of these older materials lies precisely in their ability to perform using available earth and fire, tuned by human observation.

How to think like an ancient materials scientist

When an ancient builder approached a problem, the toolbox was essentially the natural world plus fire, water, and patience. How did they make choices that led to such durable materials?

They sampled and standardized in their own way. Roman builders had favored ash pits and quarries; they knew which batches produced strong walls and which did not. Smiths watched sparks on a grindstone, listened to the ring of a bar, and chose when to fold or when to quench based on sensory cues.

They optimized for long-term behavior. In harbors, early strength was less important than whether a wall would be standing after a century of waves. In a sword, ultimate strength at one instant mattered less than how the blade would hold up to repeated sharpening and the odd impact. In coins, the question was appearance and resistance to corrosion in circulation, not tensile strength.

They leveraged environments. Romans let seawater help their concrete. The pillar's environment fostered a protective film. Skilled brass makers used the tendency of zinc to vaporize not as a problem but as a method, using sealed pots so the vapor could diffuse into copper.

They managed variability with craft discipline. Without spectrometers, the way to keep results consistent is to build controlled routines and keep the same suppliers. The shops that built the best blades or cast the brightest brasses probably had stable ore sources and lots of tuned practice.

Testing ash   Reading heat   Sealing crucibels

Where we stand now: a bridge between epochs

Modern engineers can learn from these traditions without romanticizing them. Lime-pozzolan concretes are seeing renewed interest for low-carbon construction, since they need less kiln energy than Portland cement and can offer superior durability in some environments if designed carefully. Metallurgists interested in carbide control still study historical crucible steels to understand how slow cooling and minor elements shape microstructure without modern alloy packages. Brass by cementation is not a production route now, yet understanding it enriches our grasp of diffusion processes and furnace atmospheres, knowledge that translates to vapor-phase treatments and surface engineering.

The most valuable lesson is diagnostic humility. If you cut a Roman core and do not see a particular mineral, you should not dismiss the whole category as myth; it may be a different ash or a different part of the wall. If a modern smith fails to raise a strong pattern in a crucible steel, that does not prove the ancients had a secret ingredient; it may mean the ingot chemistry or the temperature schedule needs adjustment. If a brass ingot looks dull, the crucible run may have been too hot or too long. Failures are data points, not verdicts.

Practical lessons for modern projects

- Match feedstocks to historical analogs before judging performance.
- Budget time for slow processes to reach full properties.
- Train crews to read sensory cues, not just meters, when recreating historical routes.
- Test in the real environment, not only in accelerated chambers

A closer weave: from quartz glass to seawall, from ore to pattern, from myth to mint

To see how these threads weave together, imagine three apprentices.

In a harbor yard outside Pozzuoli, the apprentice shoulders a basket of ash. The foreman shows him how to reject greenish clumps that smell wrong when wetted, how to favor the granular ash that crushes to a fine powder. He watches workers ram cobbles into a form with a rhythm that shakes the ground. He hears the hiss when water meets quicklime, and he smells the steam. He learns to live with the slow. The wall will not reach full strength in a week; it will become better for years as the sea works on it.

In a blacksmith's shop east of the Levant, an apprentice stares at a crucible freshly cracked open, a shining lens of steel inside. The master cuts off the brittle skin, throws away the corners that cooled too fast, then begins to forge the heart of the ingot at a temperature that keeps the carbides alive. The apprentice tries and fails, overheats, loses the pattern, and starts again. He learns that a degree or two in the color scale, a second or two at temperature, changes the blade's future.

In a mint near Rome, an apprentice seals pots with copper plates, powdered calamine, and charcoal. He learns that the pot must be sealed tight, that the furnace must run in a narrow range. Later, when the pot is opened and the metal poured, he taps the bar with a hammer and listens for a bright ring. Polishing reveals a yellow not unlike gold, a promised color achieved not by alchemy but by the gas that was trapped and put to work.

Three apprentices, three senses of what "advanced" means. Not miraculous, not mystical, simply a deep agreement between material, method, and purpose.

Closing the loop: what remains genuinely puzzling.

Do any puzzles remain after we strip away legend and look hard at the evidence? Yes, a few.

For Roman maritime concrete, we still do not have a universal map from ash chemistry and curing conditions to long-term mineral assemblages and their mechanical consequences. Field results vary, and while targeted experiments can replicate key features, the path to turnkey specifications that work with variable local ash is still being charted.

For crucible Damascus, there remain historical blades whose patterns and cutting performance are hard to match routinely. The variables are known in outline, yet the interaction between trace elements, carbide precipitation, and thermal cycling is sensitive. The difference between near success and the real thing can be small, which is why a handful of modern smiths, after long practice, match the old performance while many competent makers do not.

For orichalcum, the puzzle is mainly linguistic and cultural. The metallurgical process is understandable, yet the way the word moved from idealized literature to practical alloy is a reminder that stories reshape technical language. Interpreting texts demands caution.

For the Delhi pillar, the surface film's growth history over centuries, punctuated by monsoon cycles and pollution episodes, offers a sparse data record. We understand the chemistry in principle, yet the full-time series behavior of the film, down to how specific rainy seasons altered its composition, remains an open study best answered by gentle, minimally invasive analysis.

None of these puzzles demands lost continents or alien tutors. They demand respect for craft, patience for slow processes, and a willingness to read the material itself as a text that records its own making.

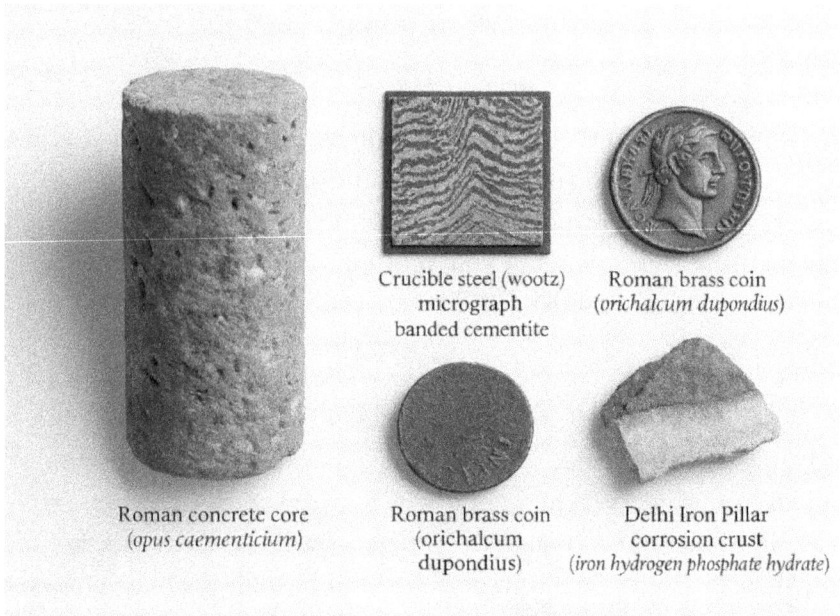

Crucible steel (wootz)
micrograph
banded cementite

Roman brass coin
(*orichalcum dupondius*)

Roman concrete core
(*opus caementicium*)

Roman brass coin
(orichalcum
dupondius)

Delhi Iron Pillar
corrosion crust
(*iron hydrogen phosphate hydrate*)

How to write the specifications, if you wanted to try

Suppose you were asked to specify a modern structure inspired by Roman maritime concrete, a blade inspired by crucible Damascus, and a demo casting of orichalcum. Here is how an engineer who respects history would write preliminary notes, always to be followed by full testing.

For the seawall, choose a volcanic ash source with documented reactive silica and alumina content similar to Campanian pozzolans. Mill to target fineness that balances reactivity and packing. Prefer quicklime addition with controlled partial slaking to allow some lime-rich clasts to persist, then verify by microscopy. Use large aggregate blocks tightly rammed to reduce percolation paths. Accept slow early strength; design construction sequence accordingly. Expose test cubes to seawater cycles to monitor mineral development over a year. Adjust water-to-binder ratio to support long-term crystal growth rather than speed alone.

For the blade, secure crucible steel ingots with target carbon slightly above eutectoid, with trace elements in the historical ranges known to promote carbide banding, then forge in a strict temperature band that preserves carbides. Use thermal cycles that reduce segregation without dissolving the carbides. Grind and etch samples to confirm microstructure before committing to full blades. Perform cutting tests against uniform fiber media, compare edge retention and toughness, and iterate. Document temperature by color charts and contact thermometers to build a reproducible schedule.

For orichalcum, run cementation trials with copper plates and well-characterized calamine or smithsonite mixtures in sealed crucibles, charcoal packed to control atmosphere. Control furnace temperature below zinc's boiling point but high enough for meaningful vapor pressure. After running, homogenize bars by short soak below melting and hot work to refine the structure. Polish and measure reflectivity and color coordinates; test corrosion in outdoor conditions, then adjust zinc uptake by altering time, temperature, and mineral grade.

These notes are not nostalgia; they are technical starting points that respect how the old routes actually work.

Final reflections: the echo in the material

If there is a message in Roman concrete, Damascus steel, orichalcum, and the Delhi pillar, it is that materials are memory. Not mystical memory, literal memory encoded in the arrangement of atoms, in the way crystals grow, in the way grain boundaries freeze or move. Ancient builders learned to write useful stories into that memory. We can still read them. When we copy the words without grasping the grammar, the results disappoint. When we learn the grammar, the echo becomes a voice we can use.

The story is not that ancient people were wizards with secret powders. The story is that they were serious experimenters who optimized for the long term, who could accept slow payoffs, and who built feedback loops with their materials. If we bring that attitude to our own century, the line between ancient and modern shrinks to the width of a crucible wall or the thickness of a passive film.

Part II: Cosmic Knowledge of the Ancients
Chapter 4: Star Maps Older Than History

If you sleep outside for a week and watch the sky without distraction, you begin to see what the ancients saw. Patterns repeat with a rhythm that feels personal. The sun rises a touch farther north each spring. The moon fattens and thins on a schedule that never misses a beat. Stars arrive on time, season after season, like expert navigators guiding a caravan across the desert. Before there were clocks, before writing, before metal crowns, there was the sky. It was the first public library, the first calendar, the first global positioning system. What follows is a careful examination of archaeological alignments, prehistoric instruments, and one remarkable bronze disk that seems to carry the night on its surface. We will treat mainstream explanations with respect, invite competing readings where the data allows, and focus relentlessly on tests that separate coincidence from craft.

The human habit of mapping the sky

Our species builds meaning by finding reliable anchors, then measuring change against those anchors. The fixed stars serve as the anchors, the moving lights serve as the variables, and the horizon serves as the ruler. Three practical needs drove ancient observation: when to plant, when to travel, and when to gather. Out of those simple needs came surprisingly advanced behavior: long baseline measurements, intergenerational record keeping, robust error control, and knowledge transfer across distances. Every place that kept people alive with farming, herding, fishing, or trade required a dependable schedule. Every dependable schedule required astronomy.

The claim that star maps existed long before recorded history does not require mystery language. It requires evidence of systematic observation, evidence that geometry-informed construction, and evidence that communities shared procedures over time. In this chapter, we will use that rubric. First, we will look at celestial alignments in stone, earth, and wood. Next, we will weigh the case for advanced astronomy in pre-recorded ages. Finally, we will study a single object, the Nebra Sky Disk, and ask what it truly records.

Celestial alignments in monuments around the world

The earth is a laboratory, the horizon is the instrument, and monuments are the marks on the scale. When the same alignments recur across different cultures and terrains, one can test whether builders targeted specific celestial events or whether we are finding patterns after the fact. Precision, repeatability, and context matter.

Stonehenge and Newgrange: solstices made visible

Stonehenge is not just a ring of stones; it is a calibrated viewfinder. The avenue points toward the midsummer sunrise, and key stones frame the midwinter sunset. The sightlines are not approximate. They operate with enough accuracy to be useful within the lifetime of the builders, and their utility survives the slow drift of the sky known as precession because solstice points are tied to the sun and the local horizon, not to star coordinates. Newgrange in Ireland takes a different approach. Its long passage and chamber admit a narrow blade of sunlight only at winter solstice sunrise, illuminating a stone recess deep inside. Both sites convert a celestial moment into an architectural event that anyone can witness. This is public science embedded in ritual.

What counts as a real alignment

Use four tests before accepting an alignment claim:
1. The line must target a significant astronomical event tied to practical cycles, for example solstices, equinoxes, or a bright star that signals a seasonal change.
2. The construction must include a sighting feature, for example a notch, corridor, paired stones, or a marked axis.
3. The precision must exceed chance. If many lines exist, apply a penalty for multiple comparisons.
4. The alignment must make cultural sense, for example match iconography, calendrical needs, or associated artifacts.

Stonehenge Midsummer Sunrise — Aerial Alignment (200 m)

Chaco Canyon and the Sun Dagger: measuring the sun with shadow

In the American Southwest, rock art at Fajada Butte receives a dagger of sunlight that crosses a spiral exactly at summer solstice midday, with companion interactions at equinoxes. The display depends on slabs that cast moving beams. Critics note that rockfalls have altered the arrangement, which complicates reconstruction. Even so, the principle is straightforward. A moving shadow can serve as a clock and a calendar. Where there is a spiral and a precise light blade that marks seasonal transitions, intentional design is a reasonable conclusion.

Chankillo in coastal Peru: a horizon observatory

A line of thirteen towers spans a ridge at Chankillo. From two fixed viewing platforms, the sun rises and sets along the horizon in a way that can be read like a vernier scale across the year. This is not a single alignment; it is a system that tracks daily motion with high granularity. When technology provides a graduated scale rather than a single yes or no sightline, we cross into the territory of sustained measurement. That is the signature of scientific thinking, regardless of the building materials.

Nabta Playa and the earliest stone circles in the Sahara

In southern Egypt near the ancient lake bed of Nabta Playa, stones form circles and alignments that key to the summer solstice and the rising of bright stars associated with the rainy season. Pastoralists who moved with the monsoon would have valued a reliable sky marker for the return of water. The simplicity of the stones does not diminish the sophistication of the reasoning: when the same star rises just before dawn at a consistent time relative to the rains, the star becomes a seasonal bell. Archaeology here suggests knowledge, not spectacle.

The Giza Plateau and cardinal precision

The Great Pyramid is aligned very close to true north. Traditional explanations show how a plumb line and paired star observations can determine a meridian with striking accuracy. This is advanced only in the sense that methodical repetition and error checking produce strong results without complex instruments. The cardinal plan also helps builders control geometry across large scales. There is no need for hidden technology to explain the feat, yet the precision does testify to disciplined observation and a culture that treated alignment as part of architectural virtue.

Angkor, Borobudur, and the sky in water

At Angkor, the main axis frames equinox sunrises and sunsets, with temple causeways doubling as sightlines. Moats serve as mirrors, turning the sky into a measurable surface. At Borobudur in Java, the stacked terraces create a walking cosmology, where sunrise alignments on certain days organize processions. These are not observatories in the modern sense, yet their plans embed celestial timing into movement and ritual, which is a practical way to teach the calendar.

Teotihuacan, the Maya, and Venus

In Mesoamerica, Venus mattered for agriculture and for politics. Buildings in key cities align with the setting or rising points of Venus on significant dates. The Dresden Codex preserves tables that predict Venus visibility across synodic cycles, and architecture appears to amplify those predictions into ceremonial timing. To track Venus well, one must record first and last appearances over many cycles, then correct for irregularities, a task that demands intergenerational data and a sturdy method for checking errors.

Göbekli Tepe and sky symbolism on the world's first hilltop sanctuary

Though earlier chapters explore its engineering, within our present theme, the question is simpler. Do the pillars and animal reliefs encode celestial patterns, or do they consolidate social memory in a sacred landscape that naturally includes the sky? The site predates pottery and metal, yet its builders crafted a place where shared observation becomes a social act. Claims that specific pillars map specific constellations remain debated. No single mapping has won consensus. The secure conclusion is that people gathered on a hill to watch, to mark, and to remember. That is the beginning of star mapping, even if the map is not a literal chart.

Evidence of advanced astronomy in pre-recorded ages

To argue for advanced astronomy long before writing, we must define advanced in operational terms. Instruments, procedures, and predictions are the core. A device, even a simple one, that extends the senses and converts motion into measurement counts as an instrument. A procedure that converts repeated sightings into a rule counts as a method. A prediction that lands close enough to plan work, travel, or ritual counts as applied science.

The three fundamental sky cycles

Solar year: approximately 365 and a quarter days, anchor for seasons and agriculture.
Lunar month: approximately 29 and a half days, anchor for tides, ritual timing, and short term planning.
Synodic cycles of bright planets: for example Venus at roughly 584 days, anchor for longer ceremonial patterns and long range signaling.

Instruments hidden in plain sight

A gnomon is a vertical stick, but as a device, it unlocks the world. Track the noon shadow through the year to mark solstices. Track the tip at midday to define true north and south. Couple a gnomon with a ring of stones, and you have a stable frame for seasonal records. Cross two sightlines at known stations, and you can mark rising and setting points with repeatable accuracy. These tools require no metal and no mathematics beyond ratios, yet they produce geometry at an architectural scale.

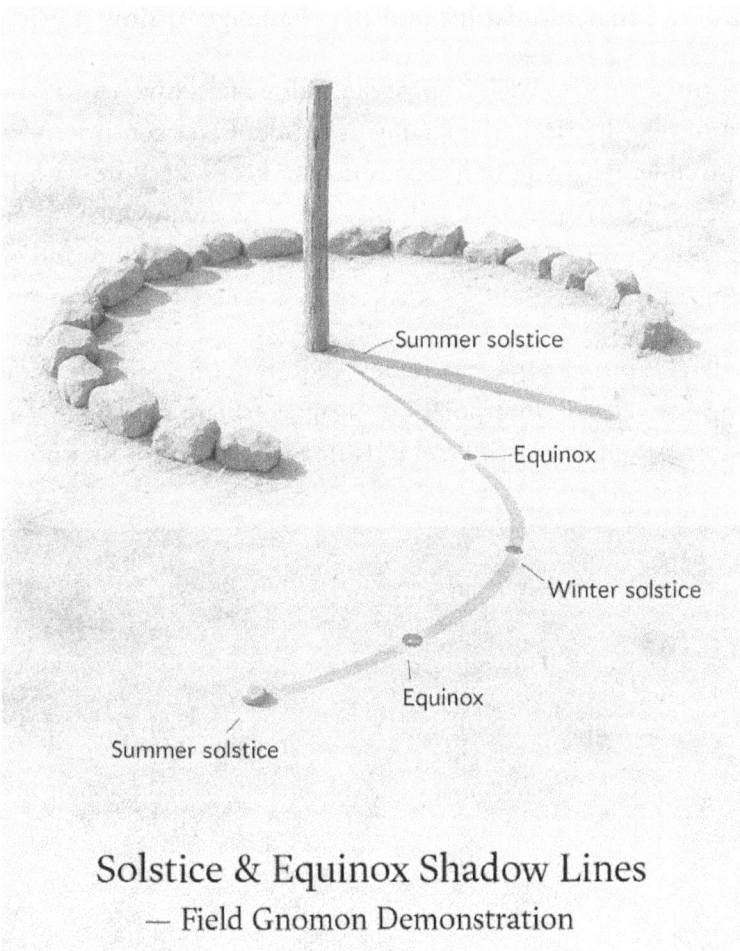

Solstice & Equinox Shadow Lines
— Field Gnomon Demonstration

Error control and the birth of long baselines

Calendrical skill grows with patient repetition across generations. Builders resurface sighting corridors, reset posts at the same coordinates, and use redundant pairs of markers to average out noise from refraction or topography. When one sees paired stones or repeated corridors with the same azimuth at a single site, that redundancy is a fingerprint of error control. A culture that teaches apprentices how to rebuild a sightline after a storm has already adopted an advanced practice: the method survives the craftsperson.

Precession, lunar standstills, and the challenge of slow motions

Precession shifts the backdrop of stars slowly relative to the seasons. Over a human lifetime, the change is subtle. Over centuries, the shift is measurable, particularly if a community keeps star lore with precise rising dates relative to seasonal anchors. The major lunar standstill, which peaks every 18.6 years, alters the extreme rising and setting positions of the moon.

Sites that capture lunar extremes require either intergenerational tracking or clever interpolation against solar markers. When a prehistoric site targets a lunar standstill with a corridor or a notch, the

Why precession matters to interpretation

1. A solstice alignment survives precession because it keys to the sun and the local horizon.
2. A star alignment drifts over centuries. An ancient corridor that once framed a specific star may miss that star today.
3. To test a star claim, reconstruct the ancient sky for the site latitude and the proposed date window, then ask whether cultural context supports the choice of that star.

burden of proof is high, yet the payoff is large. Success suggests not just casual stargazing, but organized observation over decades.

Navigation and the sky as a map

Before compasses, night navigation at sea relied on star paths and circumpolar guides. On land, the same logic helps caravans cross open steppe or desert. A society that travels far learns to map the sky to the world and the world to the sky. Polynesian wayfinders, Arab desert guides, and Arctic hunters share a common habit: memorizing a lattice of star bearings, then attaching songs, myths, and place names to those bearings. The medium is oral, the content is cartographic.

Counting, predicting, and encoding

Once a community counts days reliably, it can predict eclipses, plan long rituals, and schedule agriculture. Wooden tallies, knotted cords, and pecked rock notches serve as durable counters. When we find long counts that match lunar months, eclipse seasons, or synodic cycles of bright planets, we do not need elaborate devices to infer advanced knowledge. We need consistency. The mind is the primary instrument. The monuments, the counters, and the symbols are the external memory.

Case Study: The Nebra Sky Disk

Few objects have ignited more public imagination than a bronze plate found on a forested hill in central Europe. At first glance, it is simple. A round disk of bronze about the size of a dinner plate, inlaid with gold symbols that resemble a sun, a crescent moon, a cluster of tiny stars, and two gold arcs along the rim. Look longer, and the design becomes a compact instrument for telling time and season by the sky. The disk distills observation into art.

Discovery, context, and dating

The disk surfaced at the start of this century near Nebra in Saxony-Anhalt, reportedly with a cache that included swords, axes, and bracelets. Subsequent scientific study of corrosion layers, hammering patterns, and metal composition established a Bronze Age origin. The date generally cited is around the middle of the second millennium BCE. Some features appear to have been added in stages, which affects interpretation. The object is archaeological, not a modern forgery. That much is secure.

The circumstances of discovery were irregular, which complicates the context. That said, the chemistry of the bronze and the gold, consistent toolmarks, and weathering support authenticity. Gold trace signatures point to distant sources, likely Atlantic contacts, which fit a networked Bronze Age world where metal travelers linked regions through trade.

Nebra Sky Disk
c. 1600 BCE

What the symbols likely mean.

At center right sits a golden circle that reads as the sun. Opposite it is a crescent that reads as a young moon. Near them sits a tight cluster of seven tiny gold dots, which reads as the Pleiades, a star group that ancient observers across many cultures used as a seasonal marker. Two broad gold arcs hug the disk's rim, placed roughly opposite each other, spanning angles that match the range between solstice sunrise and solstice sunset at the latitude of central Germany. A final curved strip along the lower edge resembles a boat, a motif that many Bronze Age cultures used to picture the sun's nightly journey below the horizon.

Put together, the arrangement operates like a portable sky lesson. The sun runs along the ecliptic. The moon grows and shrinks against that path. The Pleiades cluster appears in the evening sky in autumn and vanishes in spring, a cue that herders and farmers used to time migrations and planting. The horizon arcs tell you where the sun rises and sets at solstices. The boat reminds you that the cycle repeats, renewal after darkness.

The disk as a star map and a teaching tool

A map is a model that preserves relationships. The disk does exactly that. The Pleiades cluster sits near the moon and sun, as it does in the real sky across the year. The arcs match local horizon extremes. The composition preserves the geometry of cycles without requiring a written caption. Because the elements are stylized, the disk can teach anywhere within the same latitude band. One can imagine a leader holding it up by firelight, explaining to young initiates when to expect the short days, when to watch for the return of long evenings, when to move herds, when to begin the clearing of fields.

A stronger claim sees the disk as a working instrument. In this reading, the arcs could be held level to gauge the sun's rising point relative to landmarks, or used to calibrate a standing stone line. That is plausible in principle, although the disk's weight and curvature suggest it served mostly as a symbolic standard that summarized knowledge already practiced with larger, more robust horizon markers.

Stages of modification and what they imply

> **What the Nebra Disk most securely encodes**
>
> 1. The solar cycle with solstice extremes anchored to a specific latitude.
> 2. The lunar presence as a counterpoint to the sun.
> 3. The Pleiades as a seasonal witness important to agrarian scheduling.
> 4. A maritime or riverine metaphor for cosmic cycling, for example a sky boat.

Microscopic study of the gold inlays and the hammering pattern suggests that the rim arcs and the lower boat-shaped strip were likely added after the original composition. If so, the disk's life spanned multiple generations. This would imply a living tradition that updated the object to express new emphases. First, a star map with the sun, moon, and Pleiades. Later, a teaching aid that highlights solstice arcs for horizon work. Later still, a ritual object that incorporates a sky boat motif. The object is not a static diagram; it is a palimpsest of practice.

Critics argue that staged modification is evidence against a coherent original plan. The counterargument is simple. Living instruments evolve. A working mariner scratches new marks on a favorite staff. A farmer adds a notch to a counting stick. The disk's updates are a sign of use and authority. That is what advanced knowledge looks like in a culture where memory is the archive.

Precision, latitude, and intention

The span of the arcs matches the solstice range for the site latitude within a tolerance consistent with naked eye work on a natural horizon. This is not guesswork. Someone had to stand on a ridge, watch the sun rise and set across a year, mark extreme points, and transfer that span to the disk as an arc that holds a fixed angle. That transfer reveals the key skill of horizon astronomy. The sky is the variable, the horizon is the ruler, the eye is the measure. When an artifact captures that trio with accuracy, intention is the parsimonious conclusion.

Function in society: authority, exchange, and standardization

Objects that summarize communal knowledge gain power beyond their material. The disk could have conferred authority on its keeper, who might have mediated seasonal decisions, settled disputes about festival timing, and hosted gatherings at the correct moments. Its precious metals and distant sources broadcast participation in long trade routes. Its iconography may have served as a standard that different communities recognized. When knowledge becomes portable and symbolic, it can travel faster than the builders who first derived it.

What the disk does not prove

It does not prove the existence of lost global empires, secret machines, or anachronistic devices. It does not replace the need for local observatories, gnomons, and horizon lines. It sits comfortably inside a world where people already practiced precise observation and used monuments as teaching tools. The disk is proof of synthesis. It binds star lore, solar geometry, and cultural metaphor into a compact, beautifully made object.

Final thoughts on the Nebra Sky Disk as a cultural bridge

The disk proves that ideas can travel as far as metals. Its materials imply long networks. Its design implies shared procedures. Its iconography implies a public language of sky cycles that others could read. When craft and knowledge travel together, regions synchronize festivals, markets, and migrations. The result looks like civilization in action. Not a single empire, rather a mesh of communities moving to the same celestial beat.

If there is a single lesson in these monuments and this bronze plate, it is this: advanced knowledge does not require modern tools. It requires curiosity, social investment, and patience. Our ancestors had all three. Their star maps are older than history because the sky was their first archive, and because they learned to write in light, shadow, and stone.

Chapter 5

Calendars of Eternity

There is a quiet audacity in a calendar. It claims to tame the sky, to schedule harvests and coronations, eclipses and pilgrimages, births and burials. When we imagine deep antiquity, we often imagine guesswork, yet the oldest timekeepers were not guessing. They built surprisingly exact calendars, sometimes unnervingly so, and they embedded those calendars in ritual, stone, and story. This chapter follows three threads that illustrate the scale of that achievement: the precision of ancient timekeeping in several civilizations, the mathematical logic behind the Mayan Long Count, and the controversial claims around the Dogon and Sirius, and a case study that has provoked both scholarship and speculation, the Sumerian King List with its impossible reigns. Our goal is not to sell a single explanation; it is to weigh the mainstream view against heterodox possibilities, then ask better questions.

Ancient timekeeping systems were far more accurate than expected

Agriculture punished sloppiness. If your planting calendar drifted, your fields failed, and the community followed. This pressure refined timekeeping more than any royal edict. Across Egypt, Mesopotamia, the Indus, Mesoamerica, and beyond, we find two core problems and a family of elegant solutions.

First problem: the solar year is not an integer number of days. The tropical year is about 365.2422 days. Any whole-number calendar will slide unless it is corrected. Second problem: lunar months are not tidy divisions of the solar year. Twelve synodic months give about 354.37 days; thirteen give about 383.9 days. Aligning the moon and sun required clever intercalations, periodic corrections, and sometimes nested cycles that catch drift before it becomes a disaster.

Egypt took a stark approach: a 365-day civil year, twelve months of thirty days, then five epagomenal days added at the end. No leap correction for centuries. That system drifted against the seasons, yet in practice, priests tracked the heliacal rising of Sirius, whose first predawn appearance roughly coincided with the Nile flood. Ritual astronomy acted as a seasonal reset. The civil calendar gave administrative simplicity, the sky provided agricultural truth.

Mesopotamia chose the lunar solar dance. Months began with the first visibility of the crescent. Intercalary months were added according to rules that evolved into near regular schemes. Over time, Babylonian astronomer scribes discovered repeating patterns, the most famous being the Saros cycle, about 223 synodic months, which predicts eclipse recurrences with striking reliability. Greece later adopted the nineteen-year Metonic cycle, 235 lunar months, which keeps lunar months aligned with the solar year to within a handful of hours over decades. China, India, and Mesoamerica found their own harmonics, each driven by the same arithmetic necessities.

If all of this sounds like cautious, incremental craft, it was, yet the cumulative effects are astonishing. A farmer did not need to recite

The two core tensions of premodern calendrics: 1) the non integer length of the year, and 2) the non integer relationship between lunar months and the solar year. Include the values 365.2422 days for the tropical year, 29.53059 days for the synodic month, 223 months for the Saros, 235 months for the Metonic nineteen year cycle.

ratios, but the ritual calendar that told him when to plow and when to harvest encoded the ratios for him. The temple or court carried the error budget.

Beyond expectation: precision hiding in plain sight

Scholars sometimes write as if accuracy is a modern vice and ancient calendars were polite approximations. The archaeological record and surviving texts argue otherwise.

Consider the eclipse prediction. Predicting the exact path of an eclipse requires modern celestial mechanics, yet predicting that an eclipse season is coming is a matter of pattern recognition. The Saros, 223 synodic months, about 18 years and 11 days, was identified in antiquity because tenants of sky watching kept meticulous logs. Combine that with visibility rules, and you can foresee that a darkening may visit your horizon in a given season. The refinement is practical, the underlying pattern elegant.

Consider Venus. The Maya tracked the synodic period of Venus as 584 days, a value so close to the modern mean that their Venus tables stay useful for long spans, especially when occasional corrections are applied. They were not alone in noticing planetary rhythms, yet the way the Maya integrated these numbers into a universal count, a calendar of eternity in day units, is uniquely ambitious.

Consider precession, the slow wobble of Earth's axis that shifts the background of the stars against seasonal markers over millennia. The Greeks first formalized it under Hipparchus in the second century BCE, according to conventional histories, yet there are hints, not proofs, that earlier skywatchers sensed long-period drifts. Alignments at megalithic sites, solstice corridors, and star cult calendars all become probes of long cycles when maintained across generations. Whether those hints add up to precision awareness, modern scholars argue about the details; what matters for our purpose is the mindset, the will to measure centuries with a single yardstick, and to entrust that yardstick to tradition.

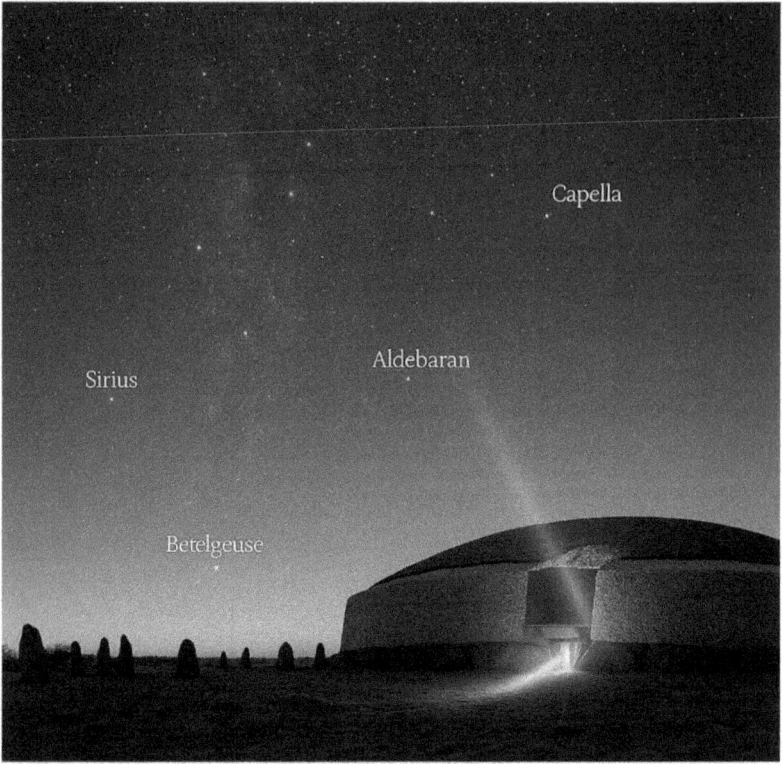

Winter Solcice Surnise

The Mayan Long Count: arithmetic as cosmology

If you want to understand ancient precision without modern machinery, study the Long Count. The Maya were not simply counting days; they were encoding cosmology in positional arithmetic.

The Long Count expresses dates as a five-place number in a mixed base: baktun, katun, tun, uinal, kin. A kin is one day, a uinal is twenty days, a tun is 360 days, a katun is twenty tuns, a baktun is twenty katuns. The system is positional, like our decimal notation, yet the choice of 18 for the step between uinal and tun converts 20 uinals to 360 days. This single design choice locks the Long Count to the solar year, not perfectly, but closely enough that seasonal rhythms remain coherent. It is a masterclass in trading neat arithmetic for calendric utility.

Because the Long Count is absolute, it can span mythic time and history without switching gears. A stela can locate a king's accession precisely, and the same syntax can place a creation era in the deep past. The celebrated base date, 13.0.0.0.0 in Long Count notation, correlates, under the widely used Goodman Martinez Thompson correlation, to 11 August 3114 BCE in the proleptic Gregorian calendar. Scholars debate correlation constants, which is healthy, yet the fact remains, you can count forward day by day from that origin and land on known historical events recorded on monuments. The calendar is not vague. It is an integer staircase across centuries.

The Maya applied the same taste for ratios to synodic cycles. The Venus table ties five synodic periods of Venus, about 2920 days, to eight solar years, a near commensurability that yields a graceful beat pattern. Errors accumulate over many cycles; therefore, the table includes correction intervals to resynchronize. This is a lesson in practical astronomy: pick a good rational approximation, monitor drift, and insert a rule that trims the drift before it becomes visible to the community.

The ritual 260-day count, often called the Tzolk'in, is not a lunar or solar year; it is a sacred cycle that interacts with the 365-day Haab to produce a 52-year Calendar Round. In modern terms, it is a least common multiple game. In lived terms, it is a matrix of meaning. A day name is a coordinate in a cosmogram that repeats only after a life-spanning interval. Fate is calendric because the calendar is not merely a clock; it is a story engine.

The Long Count structure: 1 kin equals 1 day, 1 uinal equals 20 kin, 1 tun equals 18 uinals equals 360 days, 1 katun equals 20 tuns equals 7,200 days, 1 baktun equals 20 katuns equals 144,000 days. Note that 5 Venus synodic periods equals 8 tropical years, roughly 2920 days, with occasional day corrections to maintain alignment.

The Dogon and Sirius: signal, noise, and the burden of extraordinary claims

No discussion of ancient star knowledge can avoid the Dogon controversy. The Dogon of Mali hold a rich cosmology. In twentieth-century anthropological reports, they were described as knowing that Sirius has an invisible companion with a fifty-year orbital period, and that the companion is very small and very heavy. Sirius B, a white dwarf, indeed orbits Sirius A in roughly that period, and it is neither visible to the naked eye nor imaginable to a preliterate village without telescopes, according to mainstream expectations. This led to two camps. One camp argues for cultural contamination, for example, that the information came from visitors, missionaries, traders, or colonial officials after the discovery of Sirius B by modern astronomy, then entered oral tradition and ritual explanation. The other camp suggests either a lost chain of observational or initiatory knowledge, or something more dramatic, which ranges from speculative diffusion of tools to contact theories.

Let us separate what is well supported from what is not. The Dogon celebrate the Sigui, a ritual cycle of about sixty years. This period is sometimes connected to Sirius in popular accounts, although the fit is rough if one demands an exact 50-year orbital period. The Sigui has many functions inside Dogon society, including generational renewal. Linking it strictly to Sirius B is an inference, not a consensus translation. Furthermore, the ethnographic record is thin, and the earliest detailed claims about Sirius B among the Dogon date from a period when knowledge of Sirius B had been circulating in educated circles for decades. That is fuel for the contamination hypothesis.

However, dismissing the Dogon cosmology as a single memo copied from a European astronomy book is too simple. Their star lore is internally textured; the art and masks, and terms encode multiple scales of time and being. It is possible that references to Sirius were embroidered with modern information without erasing older layers of meaning. In other words, a ritual cycle can serve social and cosmological functions, while also acting as a magnet for new technical facts that align with its prestige.

The larger lesson for our theme is methodological. Ancient calendars and cosmologies survive as braids of practice, symbol, and number. When a braid picks up a strand from contact, that does not prove the rest is a late invention. It means caution is required. The burden of proof rests on extraordinary claims, and the fairest test is prediction. A tradition that truly encodes a hidden star should yield cross-checked, time-stamped predictions that match independent observations, not only after-the-fact statements.

The difference between a ritual cycle and an orbital period. Clarify that ritual cycles can be anchored socially, agriculturally, or cosmologically, and may absorb external data over time. Emphasize the test principle: prediction precedes confirmation.

Calendars as computation: how nested cycles encode long memory

Before gears in bronze, before paper ephemerides, a calendar could be a computer. A set of interlocking cycles can approximate any irrational relation as closely as one likes, provided the culture tolerates the complexity. The Maya tolerated it. The Babylonians tolerated it. The Chinese court, staffed by calendar offices, tolerated it. Villages tolerated a simplified version, then deferred to expert keepers for high-stakes timing.

Take the nineteen-year Metonic cycle as a template. In nineteen years, you insert seven leap months to reconcile lunar and solar cycles. In practice, one distributes those seven months across the nineteen years to minimize error in festival seasons tied to lunar phases. If a tradition demands that a new year align with the second new moon after the solstice, you adjust to satisfy that constraint. The rule appears qualitative; its implementation hides exquisite arithmetic.

Or take the 52-year Calendar Round in Mesoamerica. A community that binds house dedications, market cycles, and kingly rituals to specific day name combinations will, over time, track the drift between the 365-day Haab and the 260-day Tzolk'in with lived precision. An eclipse that arrives on a day named and remembered by grandmothers becomes a mnemonic peg. Memory cheapens error.

This nested cycle logic allows deep timekeeping without metal clocks. It is also a blueprint for how complex knowledge moves in oral cultures. Modular cycles, a few correction rules, periodic resets keyed to observable events, and institutions that enforce the resets, together yield precision that surprises modern readers who equate accuracy with mechanical clocks.

Case study: the Sumerian King List and the arithmetic of the impossible

Few texts generate as much heat as the Sumerian King List. In its earliest sections, the antediluvian kings reign for astonishing spans, tens of thousands of years, then a flood intervenes, and post-diluvian reigns gradually settle into human scales. Two interpretations dominate. The mainstream view reads these numbers as mythic magnifications with ideological purpose, establishing that kingship is primordial and heaven-sent, then using inflated reigns to dignify the past and legitimize the present dynasty. The heterodox view argues that such huge numbers must encode something more technical, perhaps an astronomical scheme, a misread unit, or evidence of forgotten sophistication.

Begin with the units. Sumerian and later Babylonian mathematics used a base sixty system. Terms like soss, ner, and sar refer to 60, 600, and 3,600. If one reads the reigns that add up to multiples of these values, one might suspect symbolic totals. For example, the antediluvian total of 120 sars, 120 times 3,600, equals 432,000, a number that resonates in other traditions. That resonance tempts pattern seekers. Yet base sixty arithmetic also generates tidy round figures for administrative reasons, without implying astronomic coding. An exact multiple of a sar may simply be a way to say great age in that numeral language.

Now consider the misread unit hypothesis. Suppose the list's huge values are months, not years. Dividing by twelve moves reigns into more plausible centuries. If the numbers are lunar months, then the reigns still run long, yet they sit closer to legendary genealogies in other cultures. Scholars have explored this possibility. It does not solve every discrepancy, but it demonstrates that unit slippage can transform absurdity into allegory. Another technical reading suggests that the number words themselves were copied with place value errors. In base sixty, a single displaced sign produces a tenfold or sixtyfold change. Scribes err, especially when recopying from damaged exemplars.

A bolder reading treats the list as a veiled theoretical calendar. The impossibly long reigns, on this view, are stacks of cycles, for instance multiples of the Saros or of lunar standstill cycles of 18.6 years, or even of precessional markers. A reign of several stars might then be a constitutional assignment of a star priesthood's watch over a slice of the sky. The attraction is obvious, the pitfalls too. Without corroborating texts that explicitly map the numbers to cycles, we run the risk of reading our own yearnings into the clay. The safest compromise is to admit that sacerdotal number play was a prestige activity in Mesopotamian courts; therefore, cosmological or calendric associations would not be out of place, while still acknowledging that the political function of the list, to trace the gift of kingship through time, is primary.

What about the flood division in the list? Many cultures preserve flood memories. In southern Mesopotamia, river avulsions and catastrophic inundations occurred across historical time. A genre that uses flood as a hinge between mythic antiquity and written history is culturally natural. That hinge does not prove a single global catastrophe, nor does it reduce the list to fiction. It announces a change of register, from the age of origin to the age of record.

Hidden chronometers in architecture and landscape

Calendars do not only sit on bark paper or clay. They sit in stone. Align a long corridor toward the winter solstice sunrise, and you have a yearly clock, not because it strikes an hour, but because it verifies a date. Anchor a city plan to a cardinal direction, then check equinox shadows, and you create a civic instrument that unites cosmology with urbanism. Build paired markers to frame the extremes of the moon's standstill cycle, and you gain an eighteen-year pulse. Repeat the observation through a handful of cycles and your priest's own time in the eyes of the populace.

This is the quiet genius of monumental timekeeping. It converts the sky into a public ritual. Whether in a Mesoamerican ballcourt aligned to sunsets on particular days, a passage tomb that fills with dawn light for a few minutes each solstice, or a temple complex that stages Venus as a seasonal herald, the community experiences correctness as spectacle. The method also provides a backstop against cumulative drift in paper rules. If the calculated day for a festival does not match the beam of light that tradition insists upon, the temple has the authority to issue a correction. Calendars, in practice, are negotiated between arithmetic and architecture.

Why accuracy mattered: food, power, prophecy

It is fashionable to treat ancient astronomical accuracy as a priestly hobby. The evidence points to a triad of motives that made accuracy existential. Food, because planting and irrigation schedules depend on reliable seasonal cues. Power, because courts legitimize themselves by mastering the order of heaven, from coronations on propitious days to eclipse omens that, if foreseen, can be spun as controlled. Prophecy, because cultures grant deep meaning to cycles that repeat with enough fidelity that you can claim foreknowledge. A calendar that fails embarrasses its keepers. A calendar that anticipates becomes an oracle.

When we evaluate claims about extraordinary ancient precision, we must ask careful questions. Does the precision give a community an advantage that justifies the effort to sustain it? Do the correction rules appear in a context where someone had the authority and memory to enforce them? Is there a testable prediction that the tradition actually made? The Maya answer yes across the board. So do Late Babylonian astronomer priests. Other traditions hover at the threshold, tantalizing in hints, short on documents.

A sober reading of "advanced"

The words advanced civilization carry baggage. We imagine chrome and engines. Our subject is different. It is the use of numbers, architecture, and ritual to stabilize knowledge across time. By that standard, ancient calendars are among the most advanced devices ever invented. They are fault-tolerant because they anchor to observable events. They are maintainable, because correction rules are simple enough to transmit. They are integrative because they link sky, soil, and throne.

The mainstream historian says, with justification, that all of this evolved step by step, constrained by the limits of naked eye astronomy, and that where numbers look extravagant, ideology is the likeliest culprit. The heterodox investigator asks whether there are outliers that point beyond gradualism, and whether large numbers and long cycles signify lost technical knowledge. The right stance is neither credulity nor dismissal. It is to reconstruct mechanisms, calendars, and alignments, and to test them as engineers test prototypes. If a procedure would work as claimed, then the claim enters the realm of possibility. If it requires instruments or theories that the rest of the culture conspicuously lacks, then the burden of proof rises.

The Mayan Long Count revisited: a universal ledger of days.

Return to the Long Count for a moment, not for 2012 anxieties, but for what the system implies about historical consciousness. A society that assigns each day a unique five-place coordinate is, by definition, willing to hold both myth and memory in one grid. That willingness enables precise back referencing. An astronomer priest can say, on a day bearing such and such a name and number, Venus rose as morning star after so many days of invisibility; therefore, on the corresponding future day, Venus will play the same role. The calendar converts the sky into a ledger. Once inscribed, entries require only the next keeper to read them and apply the rule.

This is not mechanical determinism. Clouds intervene, earthquakes alter horizons, kings reorder ceremonies, conquerors impose new cycles. Yet the scaffolding remains. The day count is unbroken. A culture that sustains such an unbroken count over centuries, with documented corrections for planetary and eclipse cycles, has achieved a kind of eternity, not metaphysical, but institutional. That is the genius of the Maya and their neighbors, and it is what the phrase calendars of eternity should evoke.

The Dogon revisited: what would convince

If a tradition encodes non-obvious astronomical facts, it should be possible to extract, from time-stamped records predating modern astronomy, a set of predictions whose errors are small and whose structure matches the claimed object. In the case of Sirius B, a naked eye culture would need either a chain of indirect deductions anchored in other observable cycles, which has not been demonstrated, or evidence of optical aids, which would leave material traces. In the absence of either, the contamination hypothesis remains the parsimonious choice. That does not demean the Dogon. It reminds us that living cosmologies are dynamic, absorbing ideas across time.

If, instead, we ask a less brittle question, what cycles do the Dogon cultivate that we can verify? The answer lies in the Sigui as a social astronomical device, in agricultural timing keyed to the local sky, and in ritual art that organizes time by encoding sequences of masks and narratives. That is robust, and it fits our broader thesis, calendars as computation.

The Sumerian King List, a practical verdict

The list's large numbers are not proof of literal thousand-year human lifespans. They are proof that the number, in base sixty dress, was the language of legitimacy. By stacking sars, scribes placed the earliest kings at conceptual distances that matched their theological grandeur. They also signaled that kingship, in their understanding, is as old as the cycles they cherished. Where heterodox readings add value is in their insistence that we model the numbers and test alternative unit systems. Where they mislead is when they skip the political and literary functions of the text, the very reasons it was copied at all.

Practical takeaways for a modern reader

First, the ancients did not need metal clocks to achieve fine timekeeping. They used cycles and resets anchored to visible events. Second, accuracy was distributed. Villagers held ritual and planting knowledge, temples and courts held correction rules. Third, prestige and prophecy incentivized maintenance. Fourth, large numbers in origin stories often serve multiple roles at once: mythic elevation and, sometimes, mathematical play.

If there is a litmus test for advanced timekeeping in antiquity, it is the presence of nested cycles with documented corrections and a public architectural anchor that calibrates the rules. Egypt, Mesopotamia, Mesoamerica, China, and India passed in different ways. Claims that exceed that pattern require proportionate evidence.

Closing reflection: measuring eternity, one correction at a time

Calendars of eternity are not static. They survive by being corrigible. A leap day here, an intercalary month there, a corrected Venus table, a reset keyed to a star's first rising, these are not signs of weakness; they are signs of a living system committed to truth as the sky defines it. The most impressive thing about ancient timekeepers is not their occasional brilliance, it is their patience. They built instruments out of memory and ritual that could survive kings and droughts, and they trusted the next generation to make the small fixes that keep the great cycles in tune.

When we look for traces of forgotten advancement, we should look for that patience. Grand theories rise and fall. A well-placed slit that admits dawn light on one morning each year keeps working. A five-place day count keeps working. A base sixty table copied and recopied across centuries keeps working, even when its magnitudes shift from literal to symbolic in the minds of its keepers. Eternity, for them, meant continuity with correction.

Chapter 6

Echoes of Advanced Navigation

This chapter proceeds in three movements. First, we inspect the strongest evidence for prehistoric and early historic long-range travel, tracing its trail across genomes, crops, and cargo. Second, we walk the reader through what longitude really is, then we show how ancient astronomers could estimate it before the eighteenth century's chronometer revolution. Third, we take a close, practical look at Polynesian wayfinding, then place it alongside magnetic navigation traditions elsewhere, so the contrast clarifies the genius of each.

Evidence of prehistoric global travel

Genetic footprints across the Pacific

In 2020, a genome study tracked signals of Native American ancestry within Polynesian island populations, with the pattern best explained by direct contact between Polynesian voyagers and people from the Pacific coast of South America around the thirteenth century. The dates line up with the push of settlement into Remote Oceania, and the signal is clearest for northern South American groups, a match that makes sense given prevailing currents and winds. The work closes a long debate by showing that some encounter did take place, even if its scale was modest.

Crops tell a parallel story. The sweet potato, a South American domesticate, was in Polynesia before Europeans arrived. Botanical genetics now supports at least one prehistoric transfer from the Peru–Ecuador region to Polynesia. Experimental drift models show it is physically possible for seed capsules to cross by current, yet the linguistic fit between Polynesian names like kumara and Andean forms strengthens a human-mediated scenario. The most conservative reading is that human voyagers and currents both mattered across different episodes.

An Indian Ocean superhighway, long before charts

Another astonishing migration loop joins Borneo, the Swahili Coast, and the highlands of Madagascar. The Malagasy language is Austronesian at its core, and genome studies confirm a significant Southeast Asian component, indicating transoceanic sailing by Indonesian voyagers to Madagascar roughly a millennium and a half ago, followed by admixture with Bantu Africans on the island. This voyage is not a rumor; it is embedded in language families and chromosomes, and it demonstrates routine mastery of monsoon routes by sailors who could reliably cross thousands of kilometers.

The commercial codification of those same monsoon routes shows up in a Greek Egyptian mariner's handbook, the first-century Periplus of the Erythraean Sea. It describes when to depart Egypt to ride seasonal winds straight to the Malabar Coast, a practice connected in classical lore to the pilot Hippalus, whose name became shorthand for the discovery of direct monsoon sailing. Whatever the exact biography of Hippalus, the text is a user's manual for open ocean scheduling, not a timid coastal periplus.

Shipwrecks as data-dense time capsules

The Late Bronze Age Uluburun wreck, sunk off Turkey in the fourteenth century BCE, carried ten tons of Cypriot copper in oxhide ingots, a ton of tin, Canaanite jars with resin and glass, ivory, exotic woods, and luxury smalls. Lead isotope work traces the copper to Cyprus, and the mixed cargo maps a trade web that demanded confident open water passages and sophisticated load planning. A single merchant hull can condense the logistics of a civilization.

When texts hint at circumnavigation

Herodotus relays that Phoenician crews working for Pharaoh Necho II circled Africa from the Red Sea to the Mediterranean in the late seventh or early sixth century BCE. The most persuasive detail is their note that the sun lay to the north at noon during a segment of the voyage, which is exactly what a sailor would see in the southern hemisphere. Historians still debate the feasibility and motive, yet that observational aside has kept the tradition in the realm of the plausible rather than the fanciful.

What about the boldest claims

Sagas of Roman amphorae in the Americas or lost maps that imply global grids should be treated with skepticism until proven by context, date, and chain of custody. The absence of sustained cultural exchange signatures, such as domestic animals, pathogens, sustained vocabulary, or technologies moving both ways, keeps most transoceanic claims in the not-proven file. The contrasting cases above look different because they fuse multiple strands of evidence: genomes, crops, timetables, and freight.

Ancient use of longitude before 1700

Longitude is a time problem. If you can know the time at a fixed reference meridian and compare it to your local solar time, the difference in hours times fifteen tells you how far east or west you are. The difficulty has always been knowing that reference time while you are moving, because pendulums sulk at sea and the sky's motions are subtle. Yet clever workarounds existed long before the eighteenth century perfected marine chronometers.

The eclipse method

Hipparchus in the second century BCE explained that if two observers recorded the same lunar eclipse and noted their local time of mid-eclipse, the difference would give their longitude difference. The idea is textbook clean, although in practice, it required coordination and precise timekeeping that were hard to achieve away from observatories. The geometric insight, however, traveled well, and it seeded a family of time comparison methods.

Islamic astronomers turned insight into operations. Al Biruni and colleagues used simultaneous eclipse observations to estimate longitudinal separations of cities such as Gurgan and Ghazna, translating time offsets into degrees of arc. The same community refined tables, instruments, and procedures in a sustained program that fused astronomy with geography, long before anything like an accurate portable clock existed.

Magnetism enters the story, though not as a longitude fix.

In Song China, the compass became both an instrument and a concept. Shen Kuo described magnetizing steel needles with lodestone, the behavior of suspended needles, and, crucially, the fact that a magnetic needle does not point to true south; it is displaced slightly. That is a clear statement of magnetic declination, centuries before its regular representation on European charts. The compass changed how pilots held courses, yet declination's variability made it unreliable for precise longitude, which is why the east–west problem remained stubborn until precise celestial methods and chronometers converged.

Tables, distances, and dead reckoning

From Ptolemy onward, scholars compiled longitudes for cities using a blend of astronomical timing and travel estimates, then navigators at sea relied on latitude by sky measurement plus speed–course estimates for longitude, a practice called dead reckoning. Those estimates were disciplined by practical tools in the Indian Ocean, such as the kamal for latitude, while longitude remained an estimate, improved later with lunar distance tables that grew accurate enough by the eighteenth century to rival chronometers. The cleverness is not in pretending the problem was solved early, it is in how far early methods could go with the sky for a clock and mathematics for the conversion to arc.

Case study: Polynesian voyaging and magnetic navigation

A practical art grounded in observation

The Polynesian solution to the Pacific is a full-body synthesis of astronomy, oceanography, ornithology, and memory. Navigators used a conceptual star compass that divides the horizon into named houses, each identified with the rising and setting points of particular stars. On a voyage, the navigator did not hunt for a single needle direction; he held a sequence of bearings as the night rolled its constellations. The method is not romantic guesswork; it is a repeatable protocol taught through years of memorization and reinforced by performance. Twentieth-century revivals like Hōkūleʻa have shown that, in capable hands, the method can carry a voyaging canoe across ocean basins without instruments.

Wayfinders combine the sky with sea state. Long-period swells bend around islands and reflect, creating interference patterns that a trained body can feel through the hull. Birds commute at known distances between roosts and feeding grounds at dawn and dusk. Cloud domes mark island peaks below the horizon. The method maps a corridor rather than a razor-thin line, and position is maintained mentally with astonishing discipline.

A particularly insightful Micronesian practice, taught among Carolinian navigators, is called etak. The navigator imagines a reference island, often far off the actual track, and tracks its apparent bearing shifts against sequences of rising or setting stars. The canoe is conceptually fixed while the notional island moves; progress is divided into etak segments. This is cognitive dead reckoning using a stable external frame tied to the sky. The technique is robust because it does not require the reference island to be visible, only to be known.

What they did not need, and what others did

No credible evidence indicates that Polynesian navigators used magnetic compasses before European contact. Their instrument was the mind, trained to read the world with enough redundancy that one class of cues could validate another. By contrast, Chinese pilots integrated magnetic needles into seafaring by the twelfth century, and some northern sailors probably augmented sun and stars with polarization tricks. The famous Viking "sunstone" hypothesis proposes that Iceland spar crystals can reveal the sun's azimuth under cloudy skies by reading the sky's polarization pattern. Experiments show it can work in principle, though archaeology has yet to produce sunstones in secure Viking contexts. Together, these traditions show multiple cultures solving the same problem in different ways: keep a bearing across an ocean where landmarks hide below the curve of the Earth.

Performance, not mystique

To appreciate the level of discipline involved, consider what must be held in working memory on an inter-island passage. The navigator must know the sequence of star houses for the intended bearing from dusk to dawn, the heights and colors of those stars at different seasons, the expected wave train directions and periods for the prevailing wind regime, the likely bird species and their time windows, the cloud forms typical above different islands, and contingencies for weather that hides the sky. When experimental crews retrained on these methods and then crossed thousands of miles in the late twentieth and early twenty-first centuries, the practical verdict matched the ancestral claim: this is a scientific skill, empirical, testable, and repeatable under scrutiny.

How these threads reinforce a bigger claim

When you assemble the hard cases, a thesis emerges. People in antiquity and prehistory moved across oceans more often than our schoolbook summaries suggest. The strongest lines are in the Pacific and Indian Oceans, where winds are seasonal and predictable, stars are plentiful, and canoes or sewn ships could be built light and strong. The Pacific contact signal in Polynesian genomes, the mainland to Madagascar crossing, the Periplus schedule for monsoon departures, and the cargo spread on the seafloor off Uluburun together show a world webbed by routes that demanded precision, not luck.

At the same time, knowledge about position did not require modern devices to be sophisticated. The eclipse method for longitude, the early understanding of magnetic declination, and the later development of lunar distance tables all demonstrate that the conceptual ingredients for global grids have been on the human workbench for two millennia. The eighteenth century did not invent precision from nothing; it industrialized and miniaturized a set of astronomical and navigational insights already circulating in different forms.

Mainstream assessment, with room for anomaly

Mainstream archaeology and history accept Polynesian and Austronesian long-range feats, accept Indian Ocean monsoon sailing and its Greek and Arabic documentation, and accept the Bronze Age Mediterranean's reach. Mainstream scholarship treats transatlantic crossings before Columbus as unproven, except for the Norse in the North Atlantic, because the exchange package that would register such a link is not present. That is a high bar by design. The anomalies that make it through are those that carry multiple independent signals, which is the right way to elevate a speculation into a finding.

Heterodox questions are worth asking clearly.

Can we find further genetic traces of transient contacts in other archipelagos if sampling intensifies, for instance, in the Marquesas or the Austral islands? Could we identify short-lived settlement signatures on South American coastal sites that match Polynesian material culture tightly? Could paleoceanographic reconstructions of swell climate refine our reconstruction of plausible canoe tracks in different centuries? These are concrete research programs, and they have the virtue of being falsifiable.

Three sentences that change how we see the ancient world

Polynesians carried South American genes and crops into the Pacific before Europeans arrived.
Indonesian sailors reached Madagascar and left their language there.
Ancient astronomers knew how to recover longitude differences from shared eclipse times.

Part III: Catastrophes and Resets
Chapter 7: Fire from the Sky

On calm nights, the sky feels benign. It is easy to forget that Earth travels through a shooting gallery of rock and ice. Every so often, something big intersects our orbit, crosses the atmosphere, and releases more energy than a city has ever produced. In living memory, a space rock over Chelyabinsk, Russia, arrived without warning, the shock wave rippled across the city, glass shattered in thousands of apartments, and people bled from cuts they never saw coming. Now scale that up, not by a factor of two, but by a thousand or a million. When the sky delivers heat faster than rock can conduct it away, stone turns to glass, sand to droplets, forests to torches, and coastlines to moving walls of water. If a civilization were small, coastal, and wood-based, the record it left might fit in a shoebox of melted sand and a thin horizon of strange beads.

This chapter follows three tracks. First, what counts as reliable evidence for ancient impact events, especially those that might have intersected with human communities. Second, which geological clues point to sudden erasures rather than gentle declines? Third, a focused look at the Carolina Bays and other perplexing depressions that continue to divide researchers. Throughout, I will present the mainstream positions alongside the heterodox claims, then evaluate what each would predict and how we could test those predictions in the field.

NIGHT FIREBALL OVER COAST — AIRBURST SHOCKWAVE RIPPLES

Evidence of comet strikes and ancient impact events

Impacts and airbursts leave families of signatures. No single signal is enough, and every line of evidence has a natural lookalike. The key is convergence. When several independent indicators coincide, and the dates line up, confidence rises.

1. Shock metamorphism:

Certain minerals deform only under sudden, extreme pressure. Quartz grains can display microscopic planar deformation features that look like tidy internal lamellae. Feldspars can transform to high-pressure forms. If you see these features together, and they cross a broad area tied to a crater or blast center, you are probably not dealing with a slow volcanic process.

2. Melt glass and tektites:

When target rocks are flash melted and then thrown, they cool into glassy droplets. Tektites often form regional strewn fields, some of them enormous. Their chemistry matches the local bedrock, not volcanic magma. They can be aerodynamic, with dumbbell or splash shapes. In smaller events, you may find thin melt glass veneers fused to soil or bedrock.

3. Metallic and siderophile anomalies:

Iridium and platinum are rare in crustal rocks, but common in meteorites. A spike in iridium or platinum in a narrow layer can signal fallout from a cosmic source. The context matters: bushfires or local industry cannot generate a global platinum anomaly, although certain volcanic episodes can mimic some signals.

4. Micro-spherules and magnetic grains:

Tiny spheres of iron-rich glass, often magnetic, condense out of vapor plumes. They collect in low spots, swamps, and shallow lakes. Grain textures are diagnostic when you view them closely, yet welding slag and other anthropogenic sources can confuse the picture in young sediments. Dating and regional distribution are your friends here.

5. Nanodiamonds and lonsdaleite:

Under high pressure, carbon can reorganize into exotic structures. Reports of nanodiamonds near abrupt cultural changes are intriguing. Critics note that combustion processes can also create similar particles. Sample preparation, blanks, and independent replication are critical.

6. Craters and acoustic geometry:

A crater is not required because many explosions occur in the air. When a crater exists, its structure tells a story. Rim uplift, overturned flaps, shatter cones, and breccia lenses form a consistent geometry. Sub-ice and submarine craters complicate mapping, but modern geophysics can illuminate what silt and ice have hidden.

ANATOMY OF A SIMPLE IMPACT CRATER

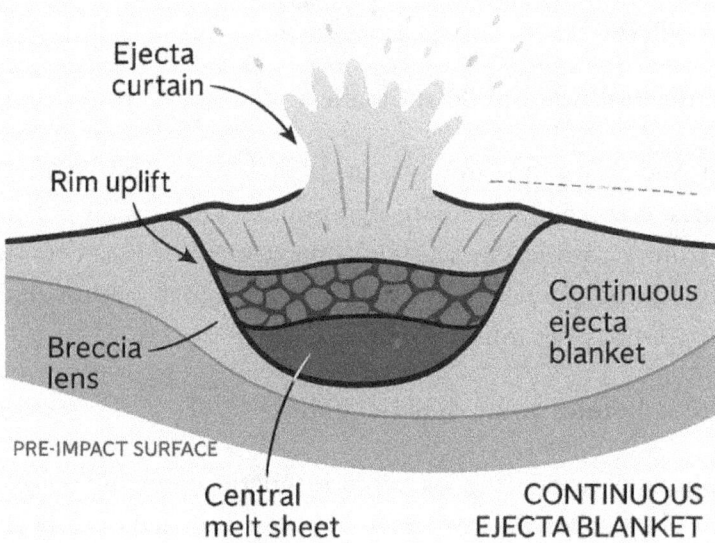

Ejecta curtain

Rim uplift

Breccia lens

Continuous ejecta blanket

PRE-IMPACT SURFACE

Central melt sheet

CONTINUOUS EJECTA BLANKET

Field checklist to evaluate an "impact" claim

- Is there a coherent event horizon that correlates across multiple sites with consistent dating?
- Are shock indicators present in more than one independent mineral phase, not just ambiguous glassy bits?
- Does geochemistry tie the melts or spherules to a single target rock package rather than mixed industrial sources?
- Is there a plausible source crater or a physically consistent airburst footprint?
- Have independent labs reproduced the key signals with blind or interlaboratory samples?

Firestones and thin horizons: a tour of candidate events

Before we leap to civilization-scale consequences, it helps to catalog the types of blows that Earth has known within or near human timescales, then ask what they did to landscapes and people.

Small but terrifying, historic airbursts

Tunguska in 1908 flattened the taiga over two thousand square kilometers. There was no crater. Trees were toppled radially, resin held microscopic spherules, and eyewitnesses reported the sky lit like sunrise. Chelyabinsk in 2013 was smaller, yet the shock wave injured over a thousand people. These two events prove an uncomfortable point: humanity did not need to know about an incoming object for it to arrive. They also show that airbursts can erase forests without digging holes, which complicates forensic work in prehistory.

Young but cratered, Bronze Age to late Holocene

The Kaali craters in Estonia, roughly mid to late Bronze Age, are a field of small impact pits with melt glass and impact iron fragments. The Henbury craters in Australia, a few thousand years old, preserve iron meteorite debris, and local oral traditions mention fire from the sky. These sites demonstrate that small cratering events occur on cultural timescales. Their footprints are local, yet their psychological imprint would have been enormous.

Pleistocene heavyweights, regional strewn fields

The Australasian tektite strewn field, about 790,000 years old, blankets a massive area from Southeast Asia to Australia. No fully accepted source crater has been located, which is a good reminder, the absence of a clean hole does not cancel the signal. That event predated modern humans in many regions, but it frames what a continental-scale glass rain looks like in the geological record.

Under ice and undersea candidates

Several putative craters, if verified, would change our timeline. Sub-ice features identified by radar in Greenland, or circular structures on continental shelves, attract attention because sea level changes and ice cover can hide scar evidence. Here, skepticism is healthy. Radar and bathymetry can trick the eye. Many circular marks are volcanic or structural domes. The burden of proof is high, the payoff is correspondingly large.

Controversial catastrophic horizons, late Pleistocene to early Holocene

Layers near the onset of the Younger Dryas cold pulse contain clusters of anomalies in some cores and soils, among them microspherules, melt glass fragments, and elevated platinum. Proponents argue for a cosmic trigger that showered the Northern Hemisphere with hot debris and soot, immediately followed by cooling, widespread fires, and abrupt biotic turnover. Critics point out that not all sites show the same package, some labs did not replicate every claimed marker, and alternative explanations like unusual volcanism or regional wildfires can fit portions of the data. A balanced reading is that an intriguing pattern exists, yet the mechanism and scale remain in dispute. We will return to the human implications after gathering more geological clues.

Geological clues that civilizations were suddenly erased

Civilizations are messy. They leave pottery dumps, charcoal floors, canals, cisterns, field walls, slag heaps, and burials. A gradual decline smears these signatures over time. A sudden reset compresses them into a horizon, sometimes a very thin one. If you want to argue that fire from the sky erased communities, you should be able to point to a few repeatable patterns.

A thin, destructive horizon with heat markers

At the settlement scale, you would expect a destruction layer that looks like a fire, but a peculiar one. Instead of slow house fires that leave thick char and recognizable collapsed timbers, you may find flash-melted surfaces, vitrified daub, and spherules embedded in roof plasters. Roofs that were thatched or reed-based would disappear completely, walls of cob or mud brick might be heat-crusted on the exterior and crumbly beneath.

Synchronous burn across a region

It is common for a valley to have a bad fire season. It is rare for several watersheds to burn in the same year without a drought or campaign of warfare. If lakes and swales across a continent hold charcoal spikes that date to within a human lifetime, and those spikes co-occur with exotic high-temperature markers, you have a candidate for a regional airburst storm or fallout event.

Abrupt abandonment followed by sterile layers

Archaeological sequences that show dense occupation, a sharp burn, then a sterile sand or silt layer can mean many things, such as floodplain avulsion or dune migration. If that sterile layer covers dozens of sites at the same time, and there is no evidence of conflict or incoming conquerors, atmospheric causes deserve consideration. Storm surges and tsunamis leave marine microfossils landward. Windborne dust layers lack marine signals. Fallout layers add geochemical oddities. The combination matters.

Coastal silence at the wrong moment

If seafaring communities clustered along low coasts during late Pleistocene sea level lows, then a later rise of about 120 meters would drown nearly every harbor, saltern, canoe shed, and fish weir on the outer shelf. A meteor strike in the ocean could cause a destructive surge even before the rise. Absence of inland sites where you might expect them, combined with submerged landscape mapping that reveals drowned river mouths with terraces and masonry like right angles, should trigger targeted dives. Most outer shelves remain reconnaissance only. That is an opportunity.

Faunal and floral whiplash

A sudden shift in pollen spectra from woodland species to pioneer weeds, paired with a spike of charcoal, implies a regional burn down. If that shift happens together with the disappearance of large mammals and the arrival of human hunting marks, interpretations will split. Was it human overreach alone, climate snapback alone, or a compound disaster that began in the sky and snowballed on the ground? Only careful dating and multi-proxy synthesis can separate those curves.

Case study: the Carolina Bays and the problem of repeating ellipses

Stand on a sandy flat in the Atlantic Coastal Plain from New Jersey to Florida, and you may be looking at land that once wore forests interrupted by thousands of shallow, elliptical depressions. Many have peat, some hold water seasonally, most align along a northwest to southeast axis, and their rims can be slightly elevated, especially on the southeast side. They range from garden scale to several kilometers long. Collectively, they are called the Carolina Bays.

The mainstream view

The dominant explanation treats the bays as the product of wind and water working on a saturated sand sheet during late glacial times. Imagine a shallow water table, strong and persistent winds, and deflation that sculpted elliptical hollows whose long axes reflect prevailing winds. As the hollows developed, waves and currents inside the ponds reworked sand into low rims. Dates from sediments inside different bays often vary, which suggests that formation and modification happened over extended periods rather than in a single afternoon of catastrophe.

Evidence for this view includes:

- The consistent orientation that matches paleo wind directions inferred from dunes in the region.
- The shallow, saucer-like depth profiles and lack of deep excavation or chaotic ejecta blankets.
- The range of ages reported from different bays fits a process that reactivated under certain climate conditions.
- The absence, in most bays, of diagnostic high-pressure shock features or airfall debris.

The heterodox view

A minority of researchers argue that the bays are secondary scars of an airburst or swarm of projectiles, possibly related to a late Pleistocene cosmic event. In one scenario, fragments struck the Laurentide ice sheet to the north. Slabs of ice and slush launched at hypersonic speed rained down across the Coastal Plain, gouging elliptical pits and throwing up rims. In another scenario, oblique shock waves dragged across wet sands and scooped them out along the flow direction. Advocates point to the systematic geometry, raised rims, and occasional reports of glassy particles in rim sands. Some versions connect the bays to wider claims about an impact-triggered climatic downturn and sudden cultural changes.

How to weigh them

Both positions make testable predictions. The eolian and lacustrine model predicts: shallow excavation with internal wave-built structures, rim sands that are indistinguishable from local source sands, and age variability that tracks hydrology and dune activity. The ballistic ice ejecta model predicts: consistent deposition of exotic clasts within rims, a narrow event window across many bays, and micro-scale shock or melt textures that are hard to fake with wind. So far, the broad survey data favor the wind and water model, yet local anomalies keep the debate alive. The right way forward is not a slogan; it is a systematic coring and microscopy program across a stratified sample of bays, paired with precise dating and blind lab intercomparisons.

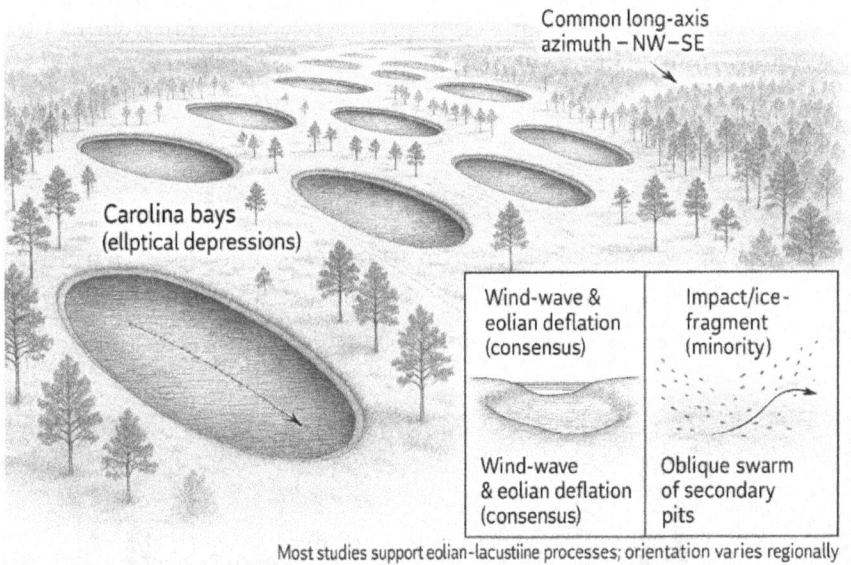

Most studies support eolian-lacustiine processes; orientation varies regionally

Other puzzling depressions

Chiemgau field, Bavaria:

Dozens of small craters in southern Germany have been presented as evidence of a Holocene impact. The mainstream counters that many of the pits are anthropogenic or related to karst processes, and that the reported melt products do not meet diagnostic standards. Lesson: crater shape alone is not enough.

Submarine circles on the shelf:

Bathymetry often reveals round forms on continental shelves. Some are volcanic cones, others are salt withdrawal pits or gas release craters, and a few could be impact-related. The tests are the same as on land: shock features in dredged cores, coherent ejecta units, and target rock context.

Lonar crater, India:

A genuine impact crater in basalt, probably late Pleistocene. Its lake hosts unique biota, and its ejecta ring is a textbook for students. Its relevance here, it shows what a clear, relatively young crater with a melt glass suite looks like, and by comparison, it underscores how ambiguous most coastal plain depressions are.

Kaali and Henbury revisited:

These fields, with meteoritic iron fragments and local narratives, emphasize that human societies can witness and remember small strikes. If a cluster of larger airbursts occurred over forested or marshy

Field checklist to evaluate an "impact" claim

- Is there a coherent event horizon that correlates across multiple sites with consistent dating?
- Are shock indicators present in more than one independent mineral phase, not just ambiguous glassy bits?
- Does geochemistry tie the melts or spherules to a single target rock package rather than mixed industrial sources?
- Is there a plausible source crater or a physically consistent airburst footprint?
- Have independent labs reproduced the key signals with blind or interlaboratory samples?

terrain at the end of the Pleistocene, physical traces might be subtle, and social memory could diffuse into myth.

Did fire from the sky erase civilizations?

The title of this book argues that advanced civilizations existed long before recorded history. To test that claim against the sky fire hypothesis, we need to separate two layers of argument. First, did abrupt, high-energy events occur during times when humans were organized enough to be called civilized by any fair definition? Second, if so, could those events have erased the material traces to a degree that convinces a modern survey archaeologist that nothing complex was there?

What counts as "advanced" before cities

Written records arrive late. Monumental stonework also arrives late in many regions. But complexity can hide behind perishable materials. Large-scale fish weirs, extensive wetland agriculture with raised fields, canalized mangrove margins, long-distance maritime exchange using sewn plank boats, and organized religious centers built of wood and earth, all of this counts as advanced if the system coordinates labor, stores surplus, and transmits knowledge beyond a single generation. The absence of stone does not equal the absence of sophistication.

What fire from the sky would do to such systems?

An airburst over a pine savanna would drive fire in sheets. Canoe sheds would ignite. Reeds would flash to ash. A sudden pressure front would tumble walls of wattle and daub. People on the water would be thrown. If the blow arrived in a dry season, fires would race and merge. If the blow landed in the ocean, a pulse of water would penetrate river mouths and salterns, lift silt, and salt fields. After the crisis, survivors would find ruined gear, ruined fields, and injured elders. Knowledge stored in memory would have to survive in the people, not in grand archives. If a second blow arrived within a lifetime, recovery would mark time. The archaeological footprint would be an interruption, not a layered archive.

Signals we should search for on the drowned shelf

- Terraced river mouths at depths consistent with late Pleistocene lowstands, with regular edges and right-angled corners that suggest human modification.
- Long linear ridges consistent with ancient shore parallel causeways.
- Piles of ballast stones that were sourced far away.
- Mud lenses with cultural plant microremains, such as phytoliths of cultivated reeds or palms, are sealed beneath clean sands.
- In select cores, the thin heat horizon is paired with marine microfossil intrusions where the surge reached inland.

Why we may have missed these signals

Most underwater archaeology has focused near shore and within well-known harbors. The outer shelves are vast. Remote sensing coverage is uneven, permissions are complex, and funding follows the familiar. Even on land, wetland sites are underrepresented because they hide beneath peat. Many survey strategies favor high ground and stone ruins. A bias toward permanence can erase the memory of perishable complexity.

The Younger Dryas debate as a civics lesson in science

The onset of the Younger Dryas, a sharp cooling near the end of the last ice age, coincides in several regions with cultural shifts, megafaunal extinctions, and burn signals. One hypothesis proposes a cosmic trigger, with one or more airbursts sprinkling the hemisphere with hot debris and soot, igniting fires, and injecting particles that altered the climate. Another hypothesis assigns the cooling to ocean circulation changes, perhaps triggered by meltwater pulses, which then cascaded into ecological stress and fires. A third camp notes that humans themselves, already widespread and inventive, could have pushed ecosystems over the edge.

What has been reported in favor of a cosmic role:

- Elevated platinum in some ice cores and sediments near the onset of cooling.
- Micro-spherules and melt glass in some sites at or near cultural transitions.
- Thin horizons of charcoal across broad areas without obvious local ignition sources.

What has been raised against it:

- Not all sites show the full package of markers, and some markers have proven hard to reproduce in independent labs.
- Dating uncertainties at the scale of decades to a century blur cause and effect.
- Alternative sources, such as unusual volcanism or remobilized industrial particles in young contexts, can imitate some signals.

What would move the needle:

- Multiple, independently dated sequences that show the same suite of high-temperature markers at the same moment across continents, paired with a plausible set of source trajectories.
- Discovery of a corresponding sub-ice or submarine crater with the right age, right chemistry, and right ejecta model.
- Blind interlaboratory replication of the most diagnostic microfeatures using standardized protocols.

Science is not a courtroom seeking a guilty verdict; it is a mapmaking exercise that adds detail across seasons. The present map shows intriguing trails, a few dead ends, and some promising ridgelines to climb.

If a reset happened, what would recovery look like

Consider a coastal culture that mastered reed boat building, tidal farming, and astronomical reckoning tied to star risings. A sweep of airbursts ignites forests inland and drives surges along the coast. The people abandon the low fields and move to the uplands temporarily. Toolkits simplify. Trade pauses. A generation later, the grandchildren build again, but this time a few kilometers inland. The old estuary is now a sand bar. The sky lore becomes myth, the story about the night the sea stood up.

Archaeologically, you would see:

- An interruption between two phases of similar culture, with a geographic shift inland.
- A temporary drop in artifact diversity and workmanship, followed by rapid recovery.
- A memory motif in oral tradition or iconography that points to fire from above or water that walked onto land. Oral tradition is not proof; it is a line on the map that tells you where to look harder.

Now enlarge the scale. Multiple coastal societies along an ocean margin experience variations of the same event within a century. Some return to the sea, others pivot to rivers. A few reinvent navigation on new terms. If writing were in its infancy, or if it lived on bark and palm leaf, the libraries would burn. If counting lived in knots on cords, the cords char. What remains are the habits of thought that can jump hosts, the ability to coordinate labor, to measure time by sky and tide, and to rebuild where the ground is still safe.

A field guide for the next decade

If we want to stop arguing in circles, we should agree on a practical program.

1. Shelf transects at paleo river mouths

Map and core the drowned deltas at depths matching late Pleistocene lowstands. Prioritize river systems that drain regions with reported high temperature markers. Look for terraces with right angles and regular stone alignments. Tag any cultural phytoliths or pollen trapped beneath sand sheets.

2. Blind replication of microfeatures

Establish a rotating program in which labs receive coded splits of the same samples and report findings without knowledge of origin. Publish detection rates for shock lamellae, nanodiamonds, and spherule textures. Make negative results visible so that the literature does not overcount positives.

3. Time-synchronized fire histories

Build a continental charcoal and pollen database with decadal bins across the late Pleistocene. Discriminate local fire regimes from regional pulses. Pair with geochemical screens for platinum group elements. The goal is to see whether fire pulses marched valley by valley or leapt across watersheds at once.

4. Wetland archaeology upgrades

Expand coring and excavation in peatlands and oxbow fills adjacent to known late Pleistocene and early Holocene sites. Many communities lived at the marsh edge. Their ruins are not foundations on hills; they are posts in mud. Train more crews to see culture in wet sediments.

5. Myth as map, used cautiously

Catalog sky fire motifs with geography and environmental context. Treat them as leads, not proof. When a motif clusters near a hypothesized airburst footprint, test the soils and cores with extra care.

Three falsifiable predictions

- If a late Pleistocene airburst swarm struck ice to the north and rained debris southward, platinum anomalies should decline smoothly with distance from the putative source, and spherule sizes should grade accordingly.
- If the Carolina Bays reflect a single ballistic event, high temperature markers of the same age should be present in a significant fraction of rims across states.
- If advanced coastal societies existed widely before the sea rose, drowned terraces should occasionally preserve straight alignments of stones sourced from inland quarries, at depths that match known lowstands.

Where this leaves the big claim

Could advanced civilizations have existed long before recorded history, then been reset by fire from the sky? The honest answer is that pieces of the picture are compatible with that idea, and pieces remain stubbornly ordinary. We have clear evidence for small to moderate impacts and airbursts on human timescales. We have debated layers with exotic markers near abrupt climatic and cultural changes. We also have reasonable, non-cosmic explanations for many of those changes, including ocean dynamics, human ecological pressure, and wind and water working quietly over centuries to sculpt landscapes like the Carolina Bays.

The strongest route forward is not to pick a team identity; it is to pick hypotheses that can be killed by data. If a claim about continental-scale destruction leaves no consistent, date-sure signature across the continent, that claim weakens. If the drowned shelf yields no cultural terraces after targeted, state-of-the-art surveys in the most promising river mouths, the coastal civilization hypothesis loses ground. Conversely, if replicated microfeatures, coherent geochemical gradients, and dated craters line up, the cosmic reset picture strengthens.

The sky has hit us. It will hit us again. Whether it wrote and erased a chapter of human complexity that we have yet to read remains an open question, not a marketing slogan. The tools to close that question exist. The will to use them, without fear of finding ordinary answers, is the real test.

This chapter set out to separate heat from light. Impacts and airbursts are real, frequent on long timescales, and dangerous even when they do not dig craters. Geological and archaeological evidence can, in principle, register their arrival, but every signal has a double. The Carolina Bays remain a test of our patience and our method. They look like a pattern that begs for a single, dramatic cause. They also behave like a landscape that wind and water could sculpt, given time and the right moisture. We should be content to test both models and keep the better one, no matter which story we want to tell.

If a fire from the sky once reset societies along the coasts and river mouths, the proof will not be an internet montage of circular ponds. It will be a concordance of dated layers, micro-scale shock features that survive peer review, and drowned terraces that still hold the handprints of planners. That is a high bar. The subject deserves nothing less.

Chapter 8

The Pole Shift Hypothesis

If you have ever stared at a world map and felt that something about the arrangement of seas and deserts looks provisional, you are in good company. For more than a century, explorers, geologists, and patient lovers of old myths have wondered whether Earth's skin has sometimes slipped, whether the blue marble we inhabit carries a memory of sudden realignments that shunted climates, drowned coastlines, and reset cultures. Careful science gives us one kind of answer. Folklore gives us another. The most productive path, and the most honest one, is to put both on the table, find the joints where they genuinely touch, and admit where they do not.

This chapter follows three threads. First, the signals in myth and geology that point to abrupt changes in latitude or climate, the sorts of things ancient storytellers described as the world tilting or the sun changing its path across the sky. Second, the practical question, how a realignment of the crust or of the whole planet's figure might have wrecked early societies that built in stone, farmed with calendars, and trusted tides. Third, a case study, a fair but rigorous revisit of Charles Hapgood's polar displacement idea, with modern physics and field data in view.

Along the way, you will see mainstream explanations placed beside strong anomalies with no hedging. The goal is clarity, not team sports. Curiosity wins when we keep both possibilities in play: either our ancestors were mainly remembering storms and gradual climate shifts that felt sudden, or they really were reporting a world that lurched.

Myths and geology point to sudden shifts in Earth's crust

What counts as a pole shift

The phrase pole shift is used in three different ways. If we are not precise, arguments pass each other and nobody learns anything.

One, geomagnetic reversals. Earth's magnetic field flips polarity on timescales of hundreds of thousands of years. Compasses would point toward Antarctica during a reversal epoch, not because the planet moved, but because the geodynamo reorganized. These reversals are real; they are mapped with exquisite detail in ocean crust magnetic stripes, and they do not move continents overnight. They can affect radiation shielding and atmospheric escape, yet they are not the subject here.

Two, true polar wander. This is the whole solid Earth rotating relative to the spin axis, because mass is redistributed. If the shape of the planet's inertia tensor changes, the body reorients to keep the largest moment of inertia closest to the equator. Imagine sliding a heavy book inside a backpack; the backpack swivels so the weight sits low. In nature, large loads of ice, vast mantle plumes, or long belts of mountains can shift the figure enough that the crust and mantle turn together relative to the spin axis. This is genuine; it has happened many times, and the rates are usually slow, measured in degrees per million years, although short spurts can be faster.

Three, crustal displacement as a separate shell. This is the Hapgood-style vision in which the lithosphere slips as a coherent unit over the asthenosphere while the deeper mantle stays put, shifting the geographic locations of the poles by many degrees within a geologically short time. That would be catastrophic. It would redraw climate belts, crack plates, and generate oceanic sloshing on a planetary scale. The mainstream view is that this kind of free sliding is physically implausible because the lithosphere is broken into plates and the asthenosphere is viscous, not a frictionless bearing. Yet it is a testable idea once you specify the timing, magnitude, and mechanism.

Three meanings of pole shift

Highlight the distinctions between geomagnetic reversal, true polar wander, and crustal displacement. Emphasize that only the last two change geography, and that only crustal displacement predicts very rapid, global reorientation with catastrophic impacts.

Myths that remember a tilted world

If dozens of cultures say the heavens changed, we should at least listen. We need not grant literal truth to every account, but it is unwise to dismiss the chorus.

In the high Andes, tales speak of a time when the sun rose in a different quarter. In parts of Mesoamerica, the Five Suns narrative remembers successive worlds, each destroyed by flood, wind, fire, or jaguars, which is poetic code for cycles of stability broken by ruin. In the Pacific, flood sagas often include details of the sea drawing back before an onrush, a detail that fits tsunami behavior. In Egypt, the idea of Zep Tepi, the First Time, carries a memory of order regained after chaos. Greek sources preserve hints that stars once rose at different points. Chinese chronicles include accounts of sky pillars breaking and rivers changing course.

Skeptical readers will say these stories are metaphors for dynastic change, for droughts, for ocean surges after quakes, or for precession, the slow wobble of Earth's axis that shifts the pole of the sky and the calendar of rising stars over twenty-six thousand years. Those explanations cover a lot. Precession alone can make a temple's alignment drift. A civilization that tracks the heliacal rising of a star will notice the calendar sliding. Over centuries, that is a slow phenomenon. Through a human lifetime, it feels like a puzzle more than a disaster.

Yet two features of the myths demand attention. First, the emotional tone. Many of these accounts are soaked in shock, not patient recalibration. Second, the coupling of sky change with water, wind, and cold. That combination, sudden realignment with geophysical violence, is exactly what a rapid true polar wander episode or an abrupt crustal displacement would feel like from the ground. The sun would start rising along a new path. The weather would go wrong. Seas would run inland and then empty. Familiar rains would fail for decades. In some latitudes, the night sky would acquire unfamiliar circumpolar stars.

We should not overfit folklore. Myth is not a seismograph. But it is a shelf where cultures store impressions of unusual events. When similarly shaped stories persist across oceans, we should at least ask whether a shared kind of event imprinted them, either a chain of great tsunamis from oceanic impacts or slides, or a climate belt shift large enough to turn garden into tundra in a single generation.

Geological clues that something moved

Myths are suggestive. Rocks keep score. If the crust or the whole solid Earth reoriented quickly, several kinds of signatures would be expected.

First, paleomagnetism. Lava cools and locks in the direction of the local magnetic field at that time. If continents rotate relative to the spin axis, the inclination of the field recorded in sequences of flows will change coherently across a region. Paleomagnetic paths already exist for many cratons, showing slow true polar wander and plate motion over hundreds of millions of years. A rapid swing would appear as a sharp kink in those paths, a many-degree jump over a thousand years or less. We do not see global, synchronous kinks of that magnitude in well-dated Phanerozoic records. That fact is a strong point for the mainstream position.

Second, ice and shorelines. If the poles moved, so would climate zones and the geography of ice. Terraces cut by waves around coral atolls, beach ridges on continental shelves, and raised shorelines around glacial lakes all provide dates and elevations for water levels. The deglaciation after the last ice maximum already left dramatic markers. Meltwater Pulse 1A raised the seas by many meters in a geological instant. That was a melt, not a whole planet reorientation. A large, rapid pole shift would likely leave a more chaotic pattern, with some areas seeing sudden regression, others sudden transgression, and a mismatch with glacio-isostatic models that assume fixed poles. Published sea level curves fit ice melt and crustal rebound quite well. That again favors gradualism.

Third, sediment disturbance layers. A global inertial event would shake basins. We would expect widespread turbidites, mass transport deposits, and mixed horizons in lakes and shelves that all date to the same century. The record we have shows many local megaturbidites tied to earthquakes and volcanic flank collapses. The distribution is not global and synchronous.

Fourth, speleothems, tree rings, and ice. Cave formations carry growth stoppages that track drought. Tree rings give annual climate. Ice cores preserve dust, acidity, and isotopes at annual resolution back through the late Pleistocene. There are abrupt events, including the onset and end of the Younger Dryas cold interval. Those are very fast climate changes, probably driven by meltwater routing and ocean circulation, perhaps with a small extraterrestrial trigger in some models. They reveal how sensitive the climate system is to forcing. They do not require a planetary reorientation, and the ice cores show continuity consistent with stable poles.

To summarize the rock evidence, what we see is a restless planet with very sudden climate swings and very large earthquakes, plus tsunamis that can ring ocean basins. We see true polar wander on slow clocks, many degrees over tens of millions of years, and we see the plate mosaic shifting constantly. We do not, in the most scrutinized late Pleistocene and Holocene strata, find a clean, global, synchronous signature of a many-degree pole shift compressed into a few lifetimes. That is a serious challenge for any rapid displacement model.

A checklist for a real pole shift in the late Pleistocene

If a rapid reorientation occurred within the last twenty thousand years, we would expect, one, global, same century kinks in paleomagnetic apparent polar wander paths, two, misfits in standard sea level curves that cannot be explained by ice melt and rebound, three, worldwide disturbance layers in lakes and shelves, four, abrupt, hemispherically coherent shifts in dust and isotopes in ice cores that suggest latitudinal climate belts moved far and fast. This combination has not been observed.

Mechanisms that could move the world

Ideas are cheap until they face physics. If we want to take reorientation seriously, we need a mechanism that can deliver torque across the lithosphere and mantle, one that respects conservation of angular momentum and the viscosity of Earth's interior.

The inertia tensor and the drive to put the heaviest belt at the equator. A spinning body wants its mass distributed so that the axis passes through the smallest moment. Earth is flattened at the poles. That bulge is part of the reason the axis is stable. If a giant mass anomaly forms away from the equator, the planet can respond by rotating the whole solid body relative to the axis, so that the anomaly migrates toward the equator. This is true polar wander. Its rate is limited by how quickly the mantle can creep and by the magnitude of the mass anomaly. That is why the background rate is modest, and why even plausible spikes would be measured in fractions of a degree per hundred thousand years, not double-digit degrees per century.

Ice sheets as movers. Kilometer-thick ice stack weighs billions of tons on the continental lithosphere. If a huge ice dome grew off-center, it would try to pull the planet's figure. Deglaciation removes that load, and the mantle flows back. This changes Earth's gravity field and can move the instantaneous rotation pole by centimeters to decimeters per year. We can measure that today. It is not the same as hauling Greenland to the equator. The scale is simply too small.

Large impacts. A big body hitting Earth can transfer angular momentum, slosh oceans, and send seismic waves through the planet. An oblique strike could, in principle, change spin state slightly. The problem is that impacts big enough to produce many degree reorientations would leave unmistakable, globally distributed ejecta layers, shocked minerals, and mass extinctions. We know the marks of such impacts. Their timing does not match the rise and fall of early Holocene cultures. Smaller impacts can devastate regions and generate tsunamis. They are a better fit for regional catastrophe myths than for a global pole shift.

Mantle dynamics and superplumes. Over very long timescales, the rise of hot mantle plumes and the fall of cold slabs can reorganize mass within Earth. That can drive true polar wander. Again, the rates are slow. Mantle viscosity is high. The Earth is not a loose ball inside a shell.

Crustal displacement as a sliding cap. This is an elegant picture, the whole lithosphere gliding over a lubricated asthenosphere by many degrees in a geologically brief episode. To work, you must posit a trigger that suddenly reduces basal coupling or suddenly applies a huge lateral shear. Advocates once suggested tidal torques from ice caps or gyroscopic effects during rapid precession changes. The math does not give enough force. Others invoked a global low-viscosity layer under the crust. Seismology does not reveal a continuous weak film that could act as a bearing. The asthenosphere is weak compared to the mantle below, yet it still resists shear strongly on human timescales. Plates also have boundaries that lock and unlock. They do not form a single, rigid bowl.

The conclusion from mechanics is conservative. The Earth can and does reorient through true polar wander, and it can change climate belts through plate drift and orbital cycles. The expected rates are slow. Suddenly, many global degree reorientations in centuries are hard to square with the measured rheology of the planet.

How a realignment, if it occurred, would destroy early civilizations

Imagine it happened. You are set down four thousand years ago in a thriving coastal city. Farmers count on winter rains that come from a reliable wind belt. Fishers read the tides and the stars. Builders set sightlines to the rising of a bright star that marks the planting day. Now move the geographic pole by 10 degrees over two centuries. This is a thought experiment, not a claim, and it shows clearly why the idea keeps returning.

First, climate belts slide. A region bathed in the descending branch of the Hadley cell, dry and clear, becomes a place under storm tracks. The monsoon arrives at a new latitude, late or not at all. On the other flank, a breadbasket that relied on gentle summers now suffers frosts. The thermal equator migrates, so rainfall patterns change. Crop calendars fail. Famine follows, then population movement. Writing that records seasonal rites becomes obsolete in a generation.

Second, seas run and return. The planet keeps its angular momentum. If the land under a new latitude band rises or falls due to isostatic adjustments, and if winds realign, landfast ice may grow in places that were once clear water. Meanwhile, a great shallow shelf becomes a trap for storm surge. Recurrent tsunamis from outer rise earthquakes along flexing plate margins chew harbors into ruins. Fishermen who once hugged a gentle continental shelf now launch into an ocean with a different temperament. Trade routes break.

Third, earthquakes for a century. As the stress field resets, faults that were close to failure let go. Subduction zones adjust to new angles. Rift zones either accelerate or stall. In a clustered century of shocks, temples crack, reservoirs drain, roads slump, and generations grow up with the ground moving.

Fourth, skies and stories. Skylines lose their landmarks. Temples that lit up with the solstice dawn now miss the beam by spans of stone. The priestly class scrambles to save a calendar that no longer fits. Some innovate, some cling to old rites, and legitimacy becomes a political question. This is not trivial. When your crops depend on communal labor and stable expectations, a broken calendar becomes a broken society.

Fifth, pathogens and ecology. Climate and wind deliver new vectors. Rodents move. Mosquitos spread. Forest pests surge. A society already stressed by failed harvests and quakes faces a novel disease. Even a modest shift in average temperature and rainfall can rewrite the biogeography of an entire region.

Could such a sequence be caused by something less dramatic than a global reorientation? Yes. Any long-run shift in ocean circulation can rewrite the climate in decades. Volcanic clusters can generate years without summers. Large earthquakes and submarine slides create tsunamis that explode onto unprepared coasts. All of these have happened. The point is not to insist on a pole shift. The point is to see why the hypothesis has held literary power. It explains many miseries with one motion. The real test is in the rocks and the timing.

Patterns in archaeology that look like resets

Archaeology is full of endings that arrive in waves. Some are clearly local: a river avulses and a city loses its port. Some are regional; a drought pushes herders across farmers' fields. Some feel larger, a pattern of change around seas that share a climate engine.

Consider shelf archaeology. The best farmland in early Holocene times often sat on floodplains that were closer to the sea. The postglacial sea level rise drowned thousands of coastal settlements. Underwater surveys on continental shelves are revealing structures, quarries, and landscapes that were dry only eight thousand years ago. This is not evidence for a pole shift. It is evidence for how bias in discovery can skew our sense of the past. A massive archive of early coastal life remains underwater and under sediment. As long as we retrieve it slowly, we will always underestimate the sophistication of early coastal cultures and overestimate the drama of their endings.

Consider calendar architectures. Alignments to solstices and stars are common. Over centuries, precession moves the sky slowly. Priests adapt with intercalations and reforms. A society that keeps adapting can treat the sky's drift as an expected puzzle. When a site is abandoned with alignments intact and undisturbed, that is often because of politics, war, trade shifts, or plague, not because the sky moved in a great leap. There are cases where alignments seem to break sharply relative to build dates. Those are invitations to recheck measurements,

Beware of missing coasts

Highlight the fact that a large fraction of early Holocene sites lie on drowned shelves. This creates a discovery bias that makes inland upland cultures look earlier or more central than they were. Emphasize the need for shelf mapping, sub bottom profiling, and targeted coring along paleo-valleys

dates, and the local horizon profile, including tree line changes and mountain snow.

Consider a sudden cold. The Younger Dryas remains a model of abrupt climate change. Rapid cooling returned for more than a millennium near the end of the ice age. Human groups adjusted. Some abandoned sites. Others changed toolkits. That change was not caused by a global reorientation. It shows how rapidly environments can swing when meltwater reroutes ocean circulation. It also shows how a stable culture can fail if it is tuned to a narrow climate window.

The reasonable conclusion is that resets are real in the human record, but their causes are diverse. The safest reading is that most resets do not require planetary gymnastics. The most interesting reading admits that people who felt the sky betray them would describe it as a moved world, even when orbital clocks and ocean currents did the work.

Case Study: Hapgood's polar displacement theory revisited

Charles Hapgood proposed that the outer shell of the Earth, the lithosphere, can shift as a unit over the asthenosphere, moving the poles to new positions within a geologically short period. He connected cartographic puzzles, memories of ice-free Antarctica, and a sense that ancient maps encode prior geographies. He imagined large ice caps off-center acting as destabilizing loads. In his view, a displacement could be tens of degrees, with the last event ending near the start of the Holocene, a timing that would allow stories of global floods to be rooted in real, rapid changes.

The appeal is obvious. One mechanism, many effects. It links myth with map, and glaciation with memory. It also assigns a starring role to Antarctica, a continent that is mostly invisible and therefore available for projections about lost coasts.

Revisiting the idea today requires four questions: mechanism, timing, evidence, and alternatives.

Mechanism. The lithosphere is not a single cap. It is a mosaic of plates, continental and oceanic, that move on the asthenosphere under slab pull, ridge push, and mantle flow. Basal drag exists. To slide the entire shell, you would need a global weak layer. Seismic profiles show a low velocity zone, which is warm and ductile, but not a lubricant. The basal shear needed to move a cap by many degrees in a short period would heat and deform the base, and that deformation would leave a fingerprint in seismic anisotropy. We do not see a global layer of that kind. We do see hot spots and plumes, and we do see channels where melt collects. Those are local, not continuous highways for whole planet slippage.

Timing. The proposal places a large displacement near the end of the last ice age. To test that, we compare paleomagnetic data from many continents. If the whole crust moved relative to the spin axis by double-digit degrees in a few millennia, we should see that sudden jog everywhere in the last deglaciation record. The data do not show it. They show the normal signature of geomagnetic field variations and secular variation, then the usual slow apparent polar wander from combined plate motion and very slow true polar wander.

Evidence. Much of the narrative built on old cartography has not survived new readings. What looked like subglacial coasts on ancient maps can often be traced to copying errors, misprojections, or composite sources from different longitudes and eras. As for Antarctica itself, deep ice cores document a continuous ice sheet spanning hundreds of thousands of years. If large sectors had been recently ice-free and then covered rapidly by a displacement that delivered the pole over the continent, we would expect obvious stratigraphic signs of a very young ice cap over fresh landscapes. The recorded layers tell a different story: long accumulation, internal flow, and climatic cycles embedded in the chemistry.

Alternatives. True polar wander is real. It can move the entire solid Earth relative to the spin axis when the inertia tensor changes. It appears to have been significant during certain intervals, particularly in the Proterozoic and early Paleozoic. It is much slower than what Hapgood envisioned. Plate tectonics explains the migration of continents over hundreds of millions of years with strong predictive success, from the fit of paleobiogeography to the distribution of earthquakes. The climate shifts of the late Pleistocene and Holocene fit well with orbital forcing, ice albedo feedbacks, changing greenhouse gases, and meltwater routing. That leaves a small space for a fast, late displacement. To occupy that space, the theory would need to predict clear, globally synchronous, physically necessary signals that we can test. So far, those predictions have failed.

There is an important nuance. Some parts of the theory asked the right questions. Why do myths of a changed sky persist? How could early calendars fail catastrophically? Why do some coasts look older than our models allow? The answers, in many cases, turn out to be drowned shelves hiding early complexity, abrupt climate changes driven by ocean circulation, and the social fragility of tightly tuned agricultural systems. The overall displacement mechanism is not required. The anomalies look less anomalous when the full set of climate and sea level data is brought to bear.

What a real pole shift would need to predict, in detail

The strongest ideas make crisp, risky predictions. Here is a clean list that any rapid displacement model must satisfy to move from speculation to a serious contender.

It must specify the magnitude in degrees and the duration in years or centuries. This determines the needed torque and the exact reorientation of climate belts. Without numbers, we are only telling adventure stories.

It must present a plausible trigger that supplies energy and changes basal coupling without catastrophically melting the asthenosphere. The trigger cannot be a tidal tug from ice; that force is far too small, and it cannot be a small impact. If the proposed impact is large enough to change the spin state by many degrees, it must also be large enough to leave a global ejecta layer and a mass extinction.

It must show that the lithosphere can behave as a coherent shell for the duration. That would require every plate boundary to either lock and move together or to adjust without breaking the shell integrity. We would expect to see a global, same-century cluster of giant earthquakes with unusual focal mechanisms. While earthquake clustering exists, the specific pattern predicted by a locked shell has not been observed in the Holocene seismic geology.

It must predict the exact latitudinal change for several well-studied regions and then match that to independent climate proxies in those regions. If a city shifted from, say, thirty-two degrees north to forty, we should see both a revised star skyline and a change in rainfall consistent with the new latitude. We have plenty of independent proxies. The match needs to be quantitative.

It must fit paleomagnetic inclination data with a coherent jump that is the same age in many places. The precision of modern radiometric dating makes this test hard to pass by accident. A global kink is either there or it is not.

When you apply this gauntlet, the rapid displacement model struggles. That does not mean the story ends. It means that the burden shifts to where the evidence actually points, toward sudden climate shifts within a stable frame and toward human vulnerability to those shifts.

The human factor, why the hypothesis persists

If the rocks are skeptical, why do people still find pole shift narratives compelling? There are at least five reasons, and understanding them helps us write better history.

First, it explains a lot with one sweep. Humans find parsimonious explanations beautiful. A single event that depresses coasts, snaps calendars, and floods valleys is a strong attractor.

Second, it gives a physical cause for mythic language. When we read that the world tilted, we want an Earth that tilted. It feels respectful to the ancestors to assume they were describing a physical world, not only using metaphor.

Third, it keeps open a possibility that early cultures were reset by something grander than regional weather. There is a sense of dignity in having been undone by the planet itself, not only by local misfortune.

Fourth, it is hard to accept how sensitive complex societies are to modest climate shifts. A few degrees and a few hundred millimeters of rain can destroy a system built on tight calendars and delicate irrigation. If your mental model of resilience is wrong, you will search for a larger cause.

Fifth, there really are lingering puzzles. Coastal cartography has anomalies. Shelf archaeology is incomplete. The timing of some cultural lurches still feels too synchronized for comfort. Those gaps invite system-level hypotheses.

The right response is to take the attractions seriously, then solve as many of the puzzles as we can with hard data. That is how respect and rigor meet.

A practical test program

Highlight a staged plan, one, assemble high resolution, radiometrically dated paleomagnetic stacks for multiple continents that span 5,000 to 20,000 years before present, two, compile a global database of synchronous disturbance layers in lakes and shelves with calibrated ages, three, overlay sea level residuals after removing glacio-isostatic adjustment to search for misfit patterns, four, integrate with stellar alignment studies at sites with secure dates. Emphasize that a single research network can execute this in five years with coordinated coring and dating.

Chapter 9

Silent Survivors

There is a moment after any great calamity when the dust settles, the sky returns to an ordinary blue, and life resumes in small, stubborn ways. People light fires again, not to signal for help, but to cook. They remember the old songs, at least the easy verses. They bury tools for another day. History rarely records this quiet interval because it is not spectacular. Yet this is where a civilization either dies or takes root again. This chapter is about the ones who kept the roots alive, the silent survivors.

We are asking three questions with care and without sensational shortcuts. First, could remnants of advanced cultures have lived on after a global or hemispheric reset, preserving fragments of high skill and transmitting them in narrow channels? Second, do myths and rituals hold inherited knowledge in forms that look like stories and ceremonies but encode practical information? Third, why do so many cultures remember small, secretive figures, goblins and dwarves, and kindred "keepers of knowledge," attached to mines, metals, clocks, and hidden treasure? We will keep the mainstream view in focus, and then we will test anomalies that deserve a fair hearing. Curiosity leads, evidence decides.

What counts as a reset

A reset is not always a single event. It can be a stack of shocks: abrupt climate swings, sea level rise that drowns coasts, volcanic winters, pandemics that empty valleys, and conflict that erases archives. The Younger Dryas cold interval, after about 12,900 years before present, was a serious shock. So was the end of that interval about 11,700 years before present, when meltwater pulses reworked shorelines and river systems. We do not need to agree on a single cause to accept that the environment changed quickly and violently in several epochs. In later eras, plague cycles, drought centuries, and ice advances have served as local resets. The key is that resets narrow the bandwidth of cultural memory. Writing disappears first, complex trade second, monumental building last, because stone keeps secrets longer than parchment.

The archaeological record is not designed to flatter survivors. The most perishable evidence goes first: wood, cloth, paper, rope, sails, and foodways. Heavy material survives better: stone, fired clay, fused metal, bone. Marine materials vanish fastest. If a knowledge tradition survives in a fishing guild or a navigator's lodge, the material fingerprint can be thin. Our question is modest: not whether a vanished global superculture existed, but whether small, instructed groups carried forward high-order techniques into the quieter centuries following catastrophe.

Preservation Bias in Archaeoeological Record

Perisahable → Durable

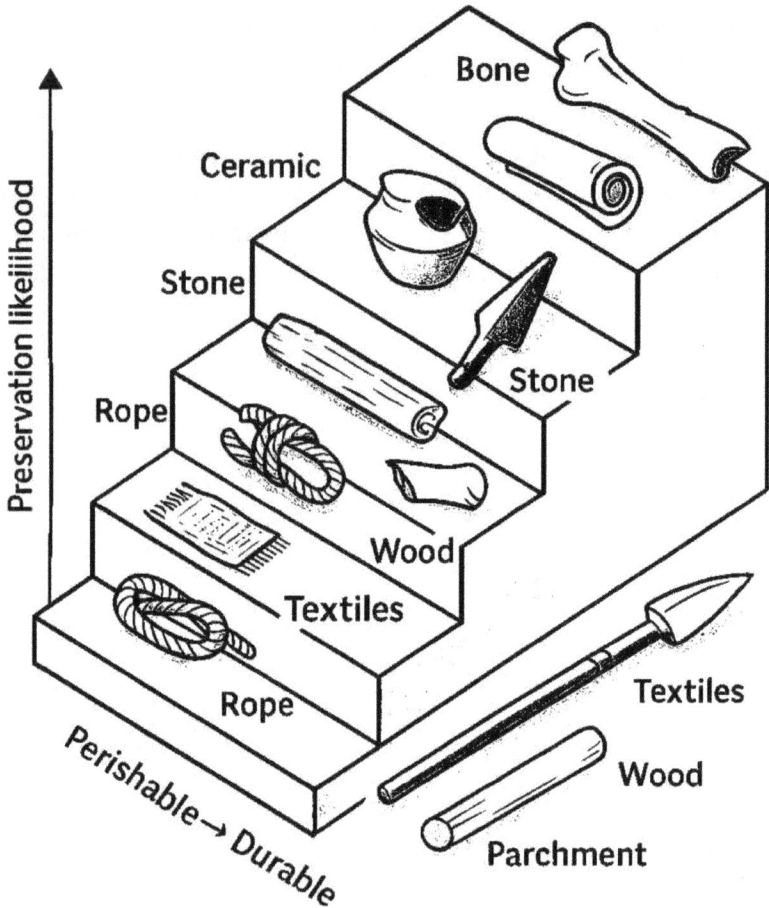

Preservation likeiihood

Bone

Ceramic

Stone

Rope

Stone

Wood

Textiles

Rope

Textiles

Wood

Parchment

Perishable→ Durable

Exceptions; arid, frozen, or waterlogged contexts may preserve organics

The channels of survival: how knowledge moves when everything else stops

After a reset, power centers fragment. Knowledge travels inside families and guilds, in ritual language, and along physical routes that remain passable when empires vanish. Five channels matter.

1. **Lineages of craft.** Metallurgy, masonry, shipbuilding, and precision timekeeping depend on tacit knowledge. That knowledge lives in hands, eyes, and sequences, not only in words. It survives through apprenticeship. The master can be illiterate yet carry a laboratory in muscle memory. That laboratory can persist across famines and border shifts.

2. **Custodial priesthoods.** In many cultures, star lore, calendars, agricultural timing, and healing practices are passed down by priests or ritual specialists. They are conservative, cautious, and secretive. They will encode seasonal corrections inside liturgies that appear mythic. The surface tells a story about a god, and the structure keeps a farm running.

3. **Maritime minorities.** Navigators and river pilots hold routes in mind. They carry songs that map coasts, bird migrations, swell patterns, and star paths. Such minorities can be mobile and endogamous, marrying within their ranks. They survive political purges by staying useful.

4. **Frontier technicians.** Miners, quarrymen, and toolmakers work where states rarely patrol. They form tight fraternities, they adopt protective myths, and they are the first to test and standardize tools. What they lack in literacy, they make up for in robustness. Their workshops look like caves of wonders to outsiders.

5. **Monastic or cloistered archivists.** In historical periods, monasteries kept books alive. In pre-literate periods, stewards of memory did similar work with bead strings, knotted cords,

counting boards, and carved tallies. When the storm passes, these stewards seed the fields of knowledge again.

Did remnants of advanced cultures live on after the reset

Evidence that is both modest and stubborn suggests this happens often. Look for regions where monumental building accelerates quickly after environmental stabilization, where precise astronomical alignments appear early in a culture, and where metallurgy begins not at the softest baseline, but at intermediate complexity. The key signatures are:

- **Abrupt precision.** When a society that appears simple builds something with clear, repeatable precision, for instance, a stone circle or a lintelled passage aligned to within a small angle of a celestial event, that is a skill spike. It does not prove inherited advanced knowledge, but it begs for a mechanism.

- **Outsized tools for the context.** When the toolkits recovered from early levels include measuring artifacts, scribing compasses, standardized drill cores, or advanced abrasives, and the surrounding domestic assemblage is basic, it suggests a specialist enclave existed within a broader rustic setting.

- **Calendrical competence.** Agricultural calendars that begin with good corrections for solar drift and lunar anomalies are rare without long observation or prior templates. If a people emerges from a reset with a calendar that already tracks a nineteen-year cycle with competence, that is a telltale.

- **Craft secrets guarded like treasure.** When myths and social rules isolate certain trades from the laity, marking smiths or masons as liminal, it can indicate that the culture perceives those trades as both powerful and dangerous, often a memory of scarce high skill after scarcity.

This is a conservative way to test the idea. We do not need to speculate about vanished continents. We can simply accept that a small cadre from a prior, more complex horizon can replant techniques without the whole apparatus of a previous civilization.

Silent Survivors, a typology

To make the evidence useful, we build a typology, not to lock people in boxes, but to separate patterns.

The Star Counters. Keepers of heliacal risings and lunar corrections. Markers of solstices and equinoxes. Custodians of planting days and ritual fasts that stabilize labor. Their artifacts are sighting stones, pecked grooves, horizon markers, and portable tally devices. Their language is metaphorical because metaphor survives when leaders are fearful of dissent and ban plain speech.

The Stone Setters. Masters of load paths, plumb, and the lesson that a thousand small stones can hold a giant lintel if the bedding is right. Their sign is the true right angle and the reliable water level. They introduce measuring rods of consistent length across valleys, which is a revolution dressed as a stick.

The Fire Breeders. Metalworkers. They control heat, air, ore, and timing. They invent rituals to cloak recipes, not because they are pious, but because passwords keep the guild alive. They can travel, because metal is welcome everywhere. They are remembered as dangerous, clever, slightly cursed.

The Water Readers. Navigators, millwrights, canal builders. They pay attention to slope, head, and flow. Their presence shows where small mills appear with sound gearing arrays, or where fish traps and weirs match seasonal runs with sophistication beyond subsistence trial and error.

The Number Bearers. Reckoners of quantity who can conserve value across time. They invent counters and accounting sequences. They mark debts on sticks, not to enrich themselves first, but to keep the clan's memory tidy when memory is thin.

None of these requires a vanished megacity. They require disciplined instruction over three masters and three apprentices in a row.

Traces of inherited knowledge in myth and ritual

When a society lacks surplus to run schools, it hides schools inside ceremony. Myths survive because they can do several jobs at once: signal group identity, entertain, and carry rules. Rituals survive because they anchor time. The question is, what within myth and ritual smells like instruction?

Encoded calendars. Stories about sky gods and trickster moons often map to real cycles. A ritual that demands counting exactly nineteen winters, or that emphasizes a sequence of five, eight, and thirteen, can point toward accumulated sky watching. This is not numerology; it is a recognition that you keep a community alive by planting on time.

Craft taboos. When smiths must remain apart, when apprentices are anointed with smoke, when the hammer must strike in specific counts, the surface looks like superstition. Underneath, it is a rhythm to enforce timing. Heat and rhythm align crystal structures and prevent failures.

Orientation vows. When a shrine must face a particular sunrise or a passage must aim at a culmination star, the rule codifies community geometry. People cannot debate the priest's preference if the star decides. The ritual cements alignment standards across generations.

Sacred numbers that do practical work. Certain numbers show up in creation stories and in measuring rods, both. Seventy two, six, twelve, twenty, three hundred sixty. They are useful divisors. A culture can gently hide unit conversion tables in hymns.

Animal masks that are also constellations. When people wear the bull, the scorpion, the bird, and the hound in a sequence that matches the sky, they are teaching where to look and when to travel. The story becomes a map by night.

The caution against overreach

Not every story is a star chart. Not every number is a code. We protect our argument by insisting on converging lines of evidence. If a myth encodes a cycle, the material culture nearby should show tools that benefit from that cycle. If a shrine aligns with a solstice, nearby fields should be planted in a pattern that takes advantage of that knowledge. The best case pairs ritual encoding with physical practice. If the two do not meet, we should withhold judgment.

Case study: goblins, dwarves, and the mythic keepers of knowledge

Across Europe and beyond, small subterranean figures haunt stories. They lurk near mines, guard hoards, and work metals. Call them dwarves in the North, kobolds in German lands, coblynau in Wales, brownies and tommyknockers among miners, leprechauns in Ireland, tomte or nisse in Scandinavia, and gnomes in early modern alchemy. Farther afield, there are earth spirits and smith spirits that occupy a similar niche. Separate traditions, different languages, similar roles. Why.

Let us take the cautious path. These figures carry three broad meanings that reflect real social history.

Memory one: the miner's world is underground, loud, and lethal. People who spend their days in gallery tunnels look small in lamp light, their faces smeared with soot, their backs bent by low ceilings. To outsiders, the workers return at dusk with eyes glittering in lamplight, shoulders hunched, speaking in codes only they understand. The leap from "the miners" to "the little people" is small. The nickname hardens into a story.

Memory two: metallurgy is a wonder and a monopoly. Taking stone and turning it into a blade that bites is indistinguishable from magic to those who do not know the steps. Early metalworkers controlled fire with bellows, watched color, and read sound. They treated furnaces as living mouths. They kept recipes inside songs. Naturally, surrounding communities endowed them with otherworldly helpers, either to praise them or to soothe envy. In many lands, the guilds helped this along because secrecy preserves value.

Memory three: treasure is a memory of risk brought home. Ore turned into ingots is a fortune you can carry. But ore is found in unpredictable pockets, and galleries collapse. Miners invented warning legends that act like safety protocols. A tapping sound means leave. Silence means stop. The friendly or cranky mine spirit expresses operational rules for survival. Over time, the rules grow faces and names.

From these three social memories, the figure of the "keeper of knowledge" emerges. In northern tales, dwarves forge gifts for gods, swords that never miss, rings that duplicate, chains that bind. In central Europe, kobolds mislead the greedy, yet they sometimes point to seams the worthy can work. In Wales, coblynau warn miners away from danger. In alchemical texts, gnomes personify the earth element, the intelligence of matter in stone. The pattern is consistent: small, secretive, powerful in narrow domains, and custodians of process.

From story to sociology: what the dwarves are hiding

Strip away the glamour, keep the functions, and you find an efficient mechanism for storing advanced craft inside hard times.

- **A guild with rules wears a myth like armor.** Outsiders respect the boundary. That boundary protects apprenticeships while the broader culture is unstable.

- **Ritual timing replaces missing clocks.** Smiths who quench at the seventh strike are really keeping time by count, a stand-in for a missing water clock.

- **The mine spirit enforces safety.** The story tells you what the manager would tell you in writing if the mine had writing. It works because it is memorable.

- **Treasure guardianship is capital control.** When a village must ration finished tools, the figure of a treasure keeper acts as a community memory of scarcity management. The hoard returns to circulation on schedule.

None of this proves contact with a vanished global advanced culture. It shows that small, disciplined fraternities can look like magic to their neighbors, especially when neighbors have lost literacy. It also shows why the memory of such fraternities persists as folklore long after the mines are silent.

The deep code inside small figures

Why are the knowledge keepers in so many tales small? Some answers are literal, and some are symbolic.

- **Literal ergonomics.** Early tunnels were cramped. Workers in such spaces appear diminutive even if they are average-sized, and a small stature is an advantage in galleries with low ceilings. Communities observing workers from a distance mythologize that trait.

- **Symbolic condensation.** A dwarf is a compact store of power. The figure compresses skill and possession into a body that fits in a story. The community sees high leverage in a small package and tells that truth as a person.

- **Children of the earth.** Smallness signals closeness to the ground. When you pull fire from ore, you look like a child privileged by the earth. This status provokes both awe and anxiety. The story reconciles both.

- **Secret custodians.** In lean centuries, the knowledge is vulnerable. A smaller figure can slip between dangers. The dwarf is also a metaphor for a small guild that survives because it is hard to catch.

Testing the keeper hypothesis with field criteria

We need criteria that a field archaeologist or an ethnographer could use: Here is a careful set.

Criterion one: tool marks that exceed the expected baseline. If a site's domestic pottery is coarse, but nearby we find drill cores with steady feed rates and symmetrical bores, or chisels sharpened with standardized bevels, we have a specialist signal. Couple that with slag heaps that indicate controlled reduction, and you have the Fire Breeders in residence.

Criterion two: site plans with hidden geometry and public ritual that points to it. If a village square is a grid or a triangle set by a consistent module, and annual processions trace its diagonals with songs about heroes who walk straight paths, the Number Bearers and Stone Setters are teaching through movement.

Criterion three: a double vocabulary. If oral accounts show stable synonyms in technical domains, for instance, three distinct words for wind that map to workable sailing decisions, while the general lexicon is volatile, a craft enclave is present.

Criterion four: export of small, high-value goods. If the site exports blades, beads, or precision fittings, and the trade network is wide even when bulk trade is absent, the enclave is living off knowledge leverage. This is the signature of a silent survivor.

Criterion five: calendar regularity tied to the local horizon.

If one shrine alignment repeats across generations while political affiliations change, the Star Counters are still on duty.

Myth as a warehouse for precision

Precision hides in repetition. Think about the ritual that repeats a number or a pattern every year. If the number carries a divisor that is practically useful, it is not an accident. For example, a festival sequence of three, six, twelve, and three hundred sixty is a memory palace for divisors of the circle. You can survey fields with simple tools if the community sings these numbers. A ritual that requires facing a specific notch on the horizon at dawn on a specific day is a community theodolite. The chorus may be about a sun god's victory, but the choreography locks the angle in place.

When we find numbers that fit real work, we treat them with respect. When we find numbers that fit no work and vary widely between villages, we treat them as decoration. Both exist. We should not be embarrassed to say so.

Why resets create keepers

A stable empire can rely on schools and archives. A post-reset society leans on guilds, shrines, and families. The reason is simple: the cost of maintaining surplus memory is high. When food stores are thin, memory must be compact, portable, and defended. The keepers are compact, portable, and defensive by design.

They are also conservative. They will refuse reforms that threaten the chain of transmission. Outsiders will call them stubborn. Insiders understand that a three-hundred-year conversation is fragile. This conservatism can slow progress. It also prevents loss. In our book, in a chapter that celebrates survivors, we give the keepers their due.

When the record talks back: mainstream cautions

Archaeology warns us not to pour meaning into silence. Absence of evidence is not evidence of absence, but it is also not an invitation to invent. We must respect stratigraphy, dating, and context. A single anomalous object cannot anchor a grand story. Clusters of practice can.

- A star-aligned passage tomb paired with a field system whose planting aligns with that same solar cue is not a coincidence. It is a practical ritual.

- A standardized blade form whose bevel repeats within a narrow margin suggests jigs and gauges, not luck.

- A compact group of imported abrasive stones at a site that otherwise consumes local materials suggests itinerant specialists, not random taste.

These are the kinds of convergences we want. If they are missing, patience is wiser than a headline.

The psychology of secrecy in hard times

Secrecy after a reset is not only about hoarding. It is about compression. When there is no paper, you compress knowledge into fewer voices. When strangers are hungry, you teach only the ones who will stay. When children are vulnerable, you wait until they can fight before you hand them the furnace recipe. This psychology explains why survivors look unfriendly in memory. They probably were. Their first duty was to carry the relay baton across a field of obstacles. Niceness was optional when the wind was against them.

Gobekli Tepe as a lesson in survival structure

A site like Göbekli Tepe, with its monumental pillars, animal iconography, and clear orientation to celestial events, sits at a hinge in human history. The site teaches us that large-scale coordinated labor and sky consciousness can flower in communities that are not yet agricultural in the classic sense. Whether or not we label this as evidence of survivors from an earlier advanced horizon, we can safely say that someone carried forward design habits, teaming strategies, and observation disciplines that outperform a simple band of foragers. The tall stones are big, but the know-how is compact, and it fits inside a few heads. That is a keeper signature.

The animal figures are not cartoons. They are labels and warnings and probably sky markers. If the scorpion and the bird appear together in a consistent placement, that points to a sequence the community knew. If the ring of pillars excludes certain motifs at certain orientations, that is a no-go map. Ritual keeps time and space honest when paper is scarce.

The Antikythera lesson, by analogy

The Antikythera Mechanism belongs to a much later world. It is a precision instrument that should not have survived, yet it did, by accident of shipwreck. Its lesson for us is not that the mechanism's makers were unique geniuses, but that high complexity can be hidden inside a small object and carried by a tiny guild. If one device can drown at sea and still tell a story two thousand years later, then how many smaller, perishable devices have gone to the bottom or to the fire? The mechanism stands as an existence proof that a pocket-sized group can hold advanced knowledge while the broader world carries on with simpler tools. This is exactly the dynamic we expect in the centuries after a reset.

The ethical dimension, keepers and communities

Keepers can be tempted to keep too much. Monopolies raise prices and stifle diffusion. Communities can be tempted to break keepers, which throws knowledge back into the fire. The healthiest path is staged release. Ritual and guild can coexist with teaching moments, where new apprentices are admitted on merit. After a reset, the balance determines how fast a culture climbs back to comfort. Stories about goblins and dwarves often carry this ethical debate. The hoarder is punished, the fair debtor is rewarded. The trickster tests the hero's humility. These are economic stories, disguised as fairy tales.

Practical signs that a survivor network crossed your landscape

For readers and researchers who want testable signs, here is a compact guide.

- **Regional standard measures.** Do posthole spacings or brick dimensions match across sites separated by a day's walk? That means a rod or cubit standard travels with a guild.

- **Non-local abrasives and pigments in micro quantities.** Small sachets of emery or haematite far from their sources point to specialist kits.

- **Reused sacred spaces with consistent orientation over centuries.** If a hilltop keeps being sacred with the same compass bearing through changing rulers, the custodian guild is steady.

- **Metal compositions that indicate recipe, not accident.** Alloy ratios clustered around functionally sensible points, such as a tin percentage that optimizes hardness without brittleness, suggest instruction.

- **Narratives that reference counting and timing in a craft context.** If the local story scolds someone for striking the wrong number of blows or turning the wheel too early in the season, those are craft rules wearing a mask.

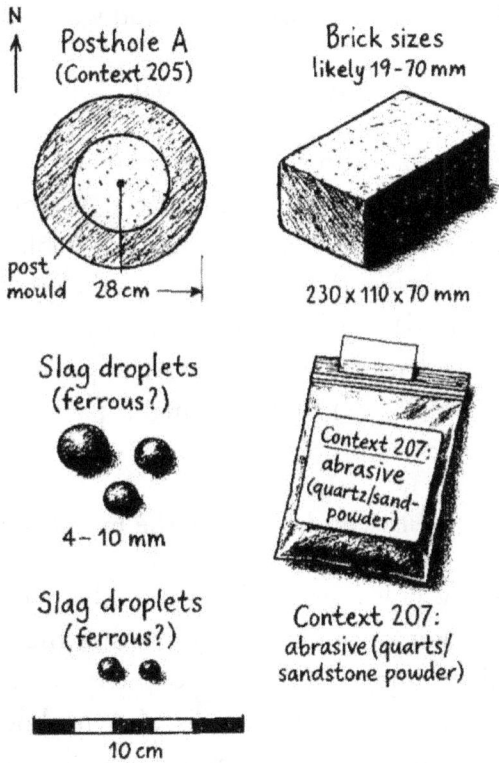

N↑

Posthole A
(Context 205)

post mould   28 cm ⟶

Brick sizes
likely 19-70 mm

230 x 110 x 70 mm

Slag droplets
(ferrous?)

4 – 10 mm

Context 207:
abrasive
(quartz/sand-
powder)

Slag droplets
(ferrous?)

Context 207:
abrasive (quarts/
sandstone powder)

10 cm

A short walk through inherited numbers

Some numbers have good reputations because they are useful. Twelve divides easily. Three hundred sixty is a circular fraction that works for surveying and astronomy. Twenty is a body count for fingers and toes. Nineteen fits the moon to the sun within a farmer's tolerance. Seventy-two appears when you notice a slow drift in star risings across three generations, if your elders told you where to look.

If a myth or ritual holds these, we do not shout Eureka; we ask who benefits. If the shepherds can move flocks on time, if the fishers set nets on the right nights, if the builders can lay out walls square without expensive instruments, then we give the story practical credit. If the numbers serve no work and the community treats them as lucky charms, then the numbers are ornaments, and we move on.

The quiet edge between myth and manual

The best manuals in hard times are songs with counts and steps. The keepers are choreographers as much as teachers. A stepping pattern that every child knows keeps the angle of a causeway stable for a century. A hymn that insists on a five-beat cadence keeps the quench timing right for blades. A circle dance that closes perfectly is a lesson in equal division. If an outsider asks why, the answer is a story about heroes. The real answer is that the causeway remains passable and the blades do not shatter.

Looking again at goblins and dwarves, the moral core

These figures show police greed. They punish theft of tools. They protect the last ingot of winter. They confuse the arrogant. For a community walking out of a catastrophe, these are not childish tales; they are governance. The small keeper is a law in shoes. Laws written on stone can be broken and forgotten. Laws worn as faces and voices travel further.

Heterodox possibility, the thin line to older horizons

Is it possible that some craft fraternities trace their lineage back before the most recent resets into older, more complex phases? If we define lineage as an unbroken, named succession, probably not. If we define lineage as a pattern that reseeds from preserved kernels, then yes. A reef regrows from fragments that cling. A culture does too. The kernel can be as small as a bag of abrasives and a song about how to count to nineteen with the moon.

We do not need to overclaim. It is enough to recognize that keeper patterns are efficient, that they appear at many times and places, and that they can carry high skill across long dark bridges.

How to write about survivors without losing the thread

We proceed with humility. We let the stones and slags and songs speak together. We do not turn one artifact into a continent. We resist the urge to make the keepers into fantasy engineers beyond their era. Their genius lies in continuity, not in extravagance. We also give them names where we can, because respect requires particularity. When a site reveals a bench with file marks that feel like a hand has just left, we pause. Someone did careful work there so that a child might grow up in a village with a mill that turns, a calendar that fits the sky, and tools that do not fail in the field.

What the silent survivors teach

They teach that complexity can be small. They teach that secrets can be ethical when scarcity rules, so long as the harvest returns to the community. They teach that a story is not a lie when it is a wrapper for an instruction. They teach that the smallest guild can carry a civilization's flame across a windy plain.

When you hear a tale about little people who keep treasure, do not rush to the gold. Ask what tool the tale protects. When you see a shrine that faces a certain dawn, do not stop at the animal carved on the lintel. Ask what field waits for the signal. When a blackened workshop floor yields a handful of slag that crunches like glass, hold it gently. Someone mixed earth and breath and time so that a blade might hold an edge when it mattered.

Part IV: The Legacy of the Ancient Echoes
Chapter 10: Technologies Waiting to Be Rediscovered

If there is one lesson echoing from the oldest stones and the deepest forests, it is this: progress is not a straight line. Knowledge moves in cycles; it gathers, shatters, and gathers again. Modern labs, satellites, and supercomputers are not the first tools to measure the world with precision; they are only the loudest. All across the archaeological record, we find practical know-how, robust design choices, and scientific instincts that were mastered long ago, then lost or minimized, and are now reemerging under new names. That is not romance; it is pattern recognition. When we learn to see these patterns clearly, we stop treating the past like a museum and start treating it like a library.

This chapter follows three threads. First, how modern science is rediscovering what ancient builders, farmers, navigators, and instrument makers already knew in practice. Second, how resonance, fields, and sound, grounded in testable physics, can reorganize a space and a nervous system in ways past cultures understood experientially, even if they lacked our jargon. Third, a focused case study, LIDAR in the Amazon, that is rewriting a continent's history and, by extension, our expectations about the scale and sophistication of tropical civilizations.

How modern science is rediscovering what the ancients already knew

Start with materials. If you want to measure a builder's intelligence, do not look only at the ornament; look at what remains standing in the rain. For two millennia, Roman harbor works and domes have shrugged off saltwater and earthquakes more gracefully than many twentieth-century structures. Recent materials science has explained a piece of that durability. Under the microscope, researchers found bright white bits, lime clasts, that act as a reactive calcium reservoir. When microcracks form and water seeps in, the clasts dissolve and reprecipitate, healing the crack. In modern language, it is a self-healing composite. In ancient language, it is just the mix that works. Replication studies point to hot mixing with quicklime, not only slaked lime, as the key that creates those clasts. The lesson is not nostalgia; it is a recipe we can now reapply to reduce maintenance, lower carbon cost, and extend service life.

Move from stone to soil. For more than a century, agronomists wrote off the Amazon as a nutrient-poor basin. Then came the stubborn fact of Amazonian Dark Earths, terra preta, black, surprisingly fertile islands of soil studded with pottery and charcoal microfragments. These patches are not accidents. They are human-engineered, built layer by layer with char, organics, and ash to lock carbon, retain nutrients, and sustain intensive horticulture. The debate over how universal or uniform these practices were is healthy, but the weight of evidence favors an anthropic origin, not a purely natural one. Modern biochar programs are catching up to that insight with controlled pyrolysis and soil-microbiome partnerships, which means a so-called cutting-edge climate technology has a family resemblance to a pre-Columbian toolkit.

Color may seem cosmetic, yet pigments are chemistry lessons frozen in time. Consider the Mesoamerican pigment often called Maya Blue. It binds an organic dye, indigo, inside the channels of a fibrous clay, palygorskite, through heat treatment that locks the chromophore into a mineral host. The result resists acids, solvents, and centuries of weathering. Conservators and physical chemists have confirmed the clay dye intercalation and the thermal thresholds that stabilize the hybrid. In other words, an ancient painter pioneered organic-inorganic nanocomposites with a kitchen kiln and a careful eye.

Metals tell a similar story. Preindustrial crucible steels, often grouped under the umbrella of wootz and later worked into pattern-welded Damascus blades, achieved a fine, tough microstructure that modern laboratories still analyze with respect. High-resolution microscopy has identified cementite nanowires and, in some samples, carbon nanotube-like features within historical blades. There is debate over how consistent those features were across time and workshops, yet the point stands: controlled impurity management and thermal cycling gave smiths a way to sculpt microstructure without a single spectrometer.

Navigation shows the same humility punch. With stick charts, star paths, wave-reading, and dead-reckoning, Pacific navigators crossed blue deserts with a mental instrument panel that rivals our electronics in conceptual elegance. No magic was needed. The ocean itself is a display if you know how to read it. The rediscovery here is not new data; it is respect for a knowledge system that encodes physics, statistics, and psychology into embodied practice.

Water management demonstrates an even broader pattern. From Andean terrace hydraulics to qanat systems that mine groundwater with gravity alone, ancient engineers chose stability over speed. The consequence is resilience. When a climate shifts or a state collapses, a gravity-fed system keeps working. Modern sustainable design is relearning that design choice. The cutting edge often looks like patience.

Oxisol vs. Amazonian Dark Earth
(Terra Preta)

Ordinary
Oxisol

Amazonian Dark
Earth (Terra Preta)

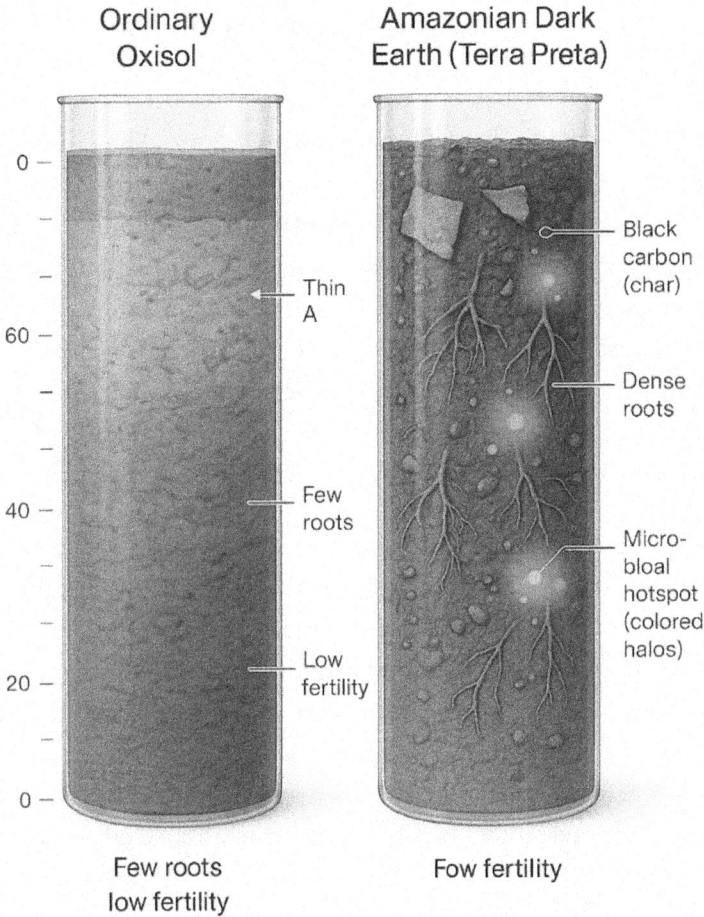

Ordinary Oxisol (left): 0, 60, 40, 20, 0 — Thin A, Few roots, Low fertility

Amazonian Dark Earth (right): Black carbon (char), Dense roots, Micro-bloal hotspot (colored halos)

Few roots
low fertility

Fow fertility

Quantum resonance, energy fields, and lost acoustics

This topic attracts more heat than light, so let's be clear. The phrase "quantum resonance" is usually misapplied in historical discussions. You do not need quantum mechanics to explain how a chamber sings or why a voice pitches differently in one room than another. You need wave physics, materials, geometry, and the human nervous system. That said, acoustics and fields are very real tools, and ancient builders were not deaf. They were experts in experience. A procession, a drum, a chant, a conch, all of these interact with stone, water, and air in ways that shape emotion.

Consider the Hal Saflieni Hypogeum in Malta. The so-called Oracle Chamber has been measured to exhibit a strong room mode near a male voice's fundamental, around 110 hertz. At that pitch, a single voice can set up a standing wave that is felt in the body and heard as an enveloping presence. Test measurements and brain studies around similar frequencies, especially when the reverberation time is long and the volumes are intimate, suggest a capacity to alter perception, not because there is anything paranormal at play, but because the auditory system is a gatekeeper to attention, heart rate, and balance.

Move to the Andes. At Chavín de Huántar in Peru, archaeologists and acousticians have documented how conch shell trumpets, pututus, and a maze of galleries with vents and canals could manipulate sound and water to dramatic effect. A droning horn in darkness, modulated by airflow, becomes both a musical instrument and an architectural organ. You do not need mystical terminology to see the point. The architecture is a sound machine, tuned to amplify, mask, and disorient in measured ways, likely in service of ritual and social theater.

Now to northern Europe for a reality check. Research teams built a precise one-twelfth scale model of Stonehenge to measure impulse responses and speech transmission. The result was practical. Voices and music inside the ring were measurably enhanced and clarified, while sounds outside were less privileged. That tells us two things. First, acoustic effects are real, measurable, and likely intentional side benefits of stone arrangement. Second, they do not require esoteric physics. They are consequences of reflection, scattering, and resonance, the same principles a concert hall designer uses today.

What about "energy fields"? The clean interpretation is electromagnetic in the literal sense, fields produced by currents, lightning, or piezoelectric effects in certain crystals under stress. There is no reliable evidence that ancient monuments were built as power plants in the modern engineering sense. There is, however, excellent evidence that builders were sensitive to environmental cues, from the way wind loads and thermal gradients travel across stones to the way water pressure communicates through an aqueduct. In that sober sense, energy is part of ancient design language.

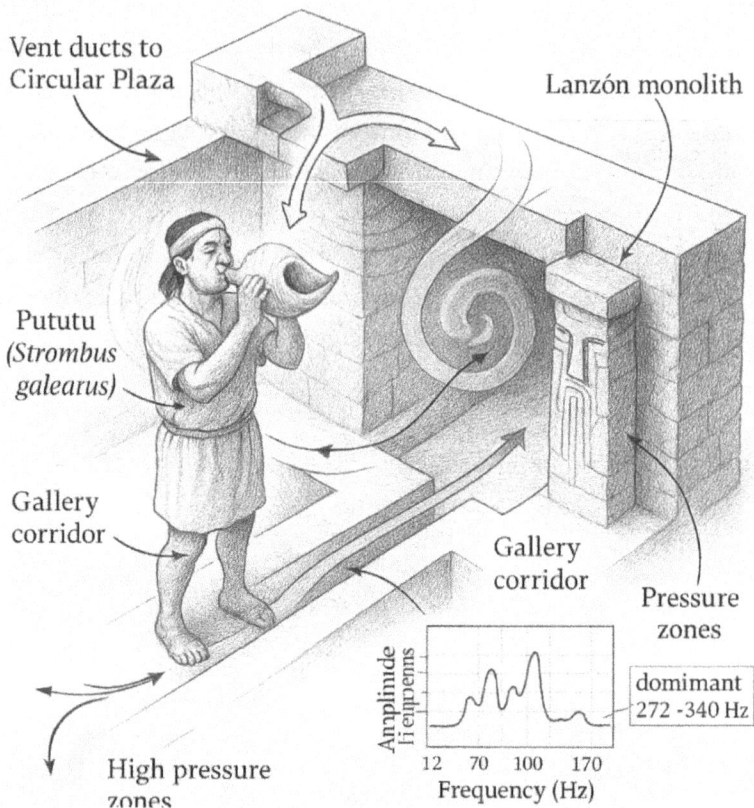

Vent ducts to Circular Plaza

Lanzón monolith

Pututu
(*Strombus galearus*)

Gallery corridor

Gallery corridor

Pressure zones

High pressure zones

Amplitude freqenms

dominant
272 -340 Hz

12   70   100   170
Frequency (Hz)

Acoustics you can test in a field visit

Clap once and listen for flutter echoes. Hum from low to high and feel where your chest voice blooms. Drop a short sine sweep on a portable speaker and measure the decay with a phone app. If the reverberation hangs at a specific pitch, you are standing in a resonant geometry. If it vanishes outdoors and returns indoors, you have a chamber effect. Ancient builders did not have FFT analysis, they had ears and time.

Case study: LIDAR and the rediscovery of Amazonian cities

If you want a single example that rewrites assumptions in real time, look at the laser. LIDAR, light detection and ranging, is a remote sensing tool that sends pulses, measures returns, and constructs a high-resolution digital terrain model. Strip away the leaves computationally, and the forest floor appears. What looked like wilderness resolves into platforms, causeways, canals, reservoirs, and mounded complexes. In the past few years, two regions in particular have forced a rethink: the Upano Valley in Ecuador and the Llanos de Mojos in Bolivia.

In early 2024, a Science paper and multiple independent reports detailed a network of settlements in Ecuador's Upano Valley, occupied roughly two millennia ago. The mapped landscape shows thousands of earthen platforms, rectilinear roadways, orthogonal planning in places, and garden-like interstitial spaces that suggest an agro-urban mosaic rather than a simple village cluster. Population estimates remain cautious, yet even conservative readings indicate an organized labor force, regional connectivity, and civic architecture on a scale that rivals many Old World contemporaries in form if not in stone. This is not a lone hilltop complex. It is a landscape of cities and fields woven together.

Two years earlier, in 2022, a Nature study using helicopter LIDAR over the Bolivian Amazon revealed a dense settlement system associated with the Casarabe culture. It documented a hierarchy of sites, including two very large centers with platform mounds, pyramidal architecture, defensive features, canals, reservoirs, and long raised causeways. The picture is not a scattering of hamlets; it is low-density urbanism across a mosaic of forest and savannah, engineered to handle seasonal flooding and to integrate agriculture with water control. Follow-up work continues to refine population ranges and settlement extent. The common thread is organization at scale.

These discoveries matter for three reasons. First, they show that cities need not look like marble and brick to be cities. Earthen architecture and living green infrastructure can sustain complex societies. Second, they demand we retire the image of a primal, untouched Amazon that only hosted small bands. People shaped this rainforest deeply, and did so with choices that balanced food, water, and biodiversity more gracefully than many modern schemes. Third, they change how we hunt for the next data. If rectilinear grids hide under the canopy in one valley, others may hide under vines elsewhere.

A few practical details help read the maps. In Upano, linear roads tend to run straight for surprising distances given the terrain, suggesting planned alignments and stable right-of-way maintenance. Clusters of rectangular platforms form nodes that resemble neighborhoods, with larger mounds likely serving civic or ceremonial roles. In the Bolivian data, the causeways stitch nodes together across seasonally wet ground, with reservoir and canal systems acting as both transport and hydraulic buffering. The texture of the terrain model, once you train your eye, is unmistakable. The pattern is too regular for geology, too integrated for chance.

Now, a word about humility. LIDAR is not a magic truth machine. It is a way to prioritize the spade and the core sample. Ground truthing, radiocarbon, ceramic typologies, paleoecology, and soil chemistry must all converge before a confident narrative stands. That process is underway. While journalists, understandably, jump to superlatives, archaeologists keep the brakes on the grand claims. That skepticism is healthy. It protects the data from misuse. Yet even with cautious language, the empirical shift is large.

How LIDAR works in five sentences

An aircraft or drone emits laser pulses at the ground and records the timing and intensity of returns. Software separates canopy hits from ground hits by classifying points at different heights. The resulting bare earth model is rendered as a shaded digital surface that exaggerates subtle relief. Archaeologists interpret rectilinear or curvilinear anomalies as cultural when they repeat, align, and match known features. The map does not prove a date or a function, it tells you where to walk, where to core, and where to dig.

What this means for "advanced civilizations" before recorded history

When you hear "advanced," you'll often picture steam engines and cranes. That definition is too narrow. A better test is complexity managed over time with knowledge captured in design. By that measure, terrace hydrology in the Andes is advanced. The self-healing trick in Roman concrete is advanced. Soil engineering in the Amazon is advanced. Conch trumpets used in tuned chambers to transform perception are advanced. In this vocabulary, "advanced" does not mean "identical to modern," it means "technically deep enough to solve recurring problems with durable, transferable methods."

The mainstream view emphasizes that many of these achievements arose independently in different regions, were rooted in local ecologies, and remained bounded by available energy sources, political organization, and trade. Heterodox views often argue for far older, globally connected knowledge systems that collapsed and were partially remembered as myth. Where can these positions meet productively? They can meet at the site level with testable predictions. If a supposed tradition claimed knowledge of precise acoustical design, we can test resonance in a chamber. If a story implies large-scale gridded agriculture in a forested region, we can fly LIDAR and core the soil. When the data supports sophistication, the mainstream absorbs it. When it does not, the burden of proof remains.

Fifteen technologies and practices that are, in effect, waiting to be rediscovered

I am not listing gadgets. I am naming design moves that work, that we understand mechanistically, and that we can adapt at scale.

1. Hot-mixed lime concretes with self-healing capacity. The recipe is not a secret anymore. The challenge is code adoption and industrial scaling with modern aggregates. Start with marine works where life-cycle maintenance kills budgets.

2. Earthen urbanism. Cities do not have to sprawl in concrete. Raised fields, causeways, and mounded platforms can create walkable drainage-smart fabrics that handle seasonal water like a friend rather than a threat. The Bolivian and Ecuadorian examples show templates.

3. Biochar-based soil building. We can create durable carbon sinks that also raise yields and buffer pH. The modern twist is monitoring and fair crediting, so farmers are paid for ecological services.

4. Acoustic architecture by intent. From clinics to transit stations, small shifts in shape and surface can tame stress and sharpen speech intelligibility. Prehistory offers case studies in visceral sound design that we can translate without mysticism.

5. Durable pigments from hybrid organics and minerals. The Maya Blue principle, organic molecules stabilized in mineral hosts, is a playbook for non-toxic, long-lived coatings.

6. Low-tech, high-reliability hydraulics. Gravity and capillarity never lose power. Qanat logic can inspire modern off-grid water delivery where pumps are fragile and power is scarce.

7. Terraced agrohydrology. If you farm slopes, you can either fight gravity or ride it. Ancient terraces ride it. Modern terrace retrofits, with geotextiles and sensor feedback, are even better.

8. Redundant analog computing for dirty environments. The spirit of geared calculation, as seen in famous Hellenic mechanisms, is not to replace microchips; it is to add resilience with tactile, inspectable systems when EMI, dust, or radiation make electronics twitchy.

9. Timber joints that move rather than crack. Traditional joinery techniques accept seasonal movement. Combined with modern analysis, they can extend timber lifespans without coatings that fail.

10. Stone as a tuned thermal battery. Thick masonry stabilizes diurnal swings. With modern phase change inserts and night purging, old walls become quiet energy devices.

11. Green corridors as infrastructure, not ornament. Ancient causeways often doubled as berms and ecological edges. Urban designers can copy that multifunctionality today.

12. Local clay composites for shelter. Properly designed earthen plasters and compressed earth blocks can achieve high-performance envelopes with low embodied carbon.

13. Wind capture without moving parts. Traditional wind scoops and courtyards modulate temperature and purify air. Combine them with passive filtration, and you get comfort with almost no energy.

14. Living floodplains. Treat seasonal water like a scheduling problem, not an enemy. The Amazonian precedent tells us you can farm and move through amphibious environments if you design for the rhythm rather than against it.

15. Ritual performance as a civic technology. This may sound soft, yet the acoustics of shared ceremony do political work. Spaces that synchronize breath and attention build social trust. In a fraying civic sphere, that is not cosmetic.

Objections answered, without drama.

"You are just romanticizing the past." I am romantic about evidence. Where the data speaks clearly, I listen. Where it does not, I say so.

LIDAR maps, thin sections of mortar, Raman spectra of pigments, and measured reverberation times are not nostalgia; they are quantification.

"If these techniques were so good, why were they lost?" Knowledge is fragile. Trade routes shift, a key ore source runs out, a scribe dies without an apprentice, and a war interrupts a guild. Sometimes a "superior" technology outcompetes an older one on speed or cost, even if durability suffers. The Roman lime trick did not vanish because it failed; it vanished because the social system that supported it fractured, and then Portland cement rose with industrialization.

"Calling earthen settlements 'cities' stretches the word." Only if you define a city by stone. If you define it by population clustering, infrastructure, labor organization, and administrative or ceremonial architecture, the low-density urban fabrics in the Amazon qualify. The scientific literature itself uses that language with caution and care.

"Quantum resonance explains everything; modern science is too limited." The measurable acoustic and electromagnetic phenomena we discuss here are sufficient. Bringing in quantum language, where classical wave theory explains the observations, does not add accuracy. It adds confusion. The marvel is that classical physics and careful craft were enough.

Field guide for the next decade of rediscoveries

Where should we look next? Start with places where canopy and mud hide regularity. The lowlands of western Amazonia are obvious candidates for further LIDAR passes. So are parts of New Guinea, Borneo, and the Congo Basin. Anywhere flood pulses mix with alluvium, ancient engineers likely experimented with raised fields and causeways. Expect surprises along mid-elevation Andean foothills and the edges of shield regions in South America and Africa, where soils are poor yet terrace logic could thrive.

On the materials side, assume there are other "blind recipes" waiting in mortar joints and plaster layers. Systematic microanalysis of lime mixes outside imperial capitals, along roads, and in rural sanctuaries will likely uncover regional variants that adapted to local aggregates, ash chemistries, and humidity. That is not trivial. Those variants could yield modern formulations with better performance in specific climates.

Acoustically, expect a wave of careful measurements across megalithic chambers, rock-cut tombs, and cave complexes. The right protocol is simple. Laser scan the geometry, compute room modes, measure on site, then replicate with a physical scale model where access is limited or fragile. Where the data shows a strong mode aligned with human vocal ranges, treat it as a design, whether by intent or by iterative selection. The builders did not need formulas to select a pitch. They had voices and feedback.

A brief, grounded look at "energy fields" through the body

Let's anchor the physiology. Low-frequency sound, below about 200 hertz, couples strongly to the chest and abdomen. Sustained tones in that band can nudge breathing and heart rate through vagal pathways. Reverberation adds a sense of presence because the early reflections within 50 to 80 milliseconds reinforce the direct sound and trick the auditory cortex into attributing size and importance to the source. Builders did not need to quantify any of this. They only needed to notice that a chant at one pitch moved people more than another, then carve the space to support that pitch. The Hypogeum example, with a strong response around 110 hertz, is a clean demonstration of that loop: space selects pitch, pitch selects feeling.

Reading an Amazonian LIDAR image in two minutes

Look for straight lines that ignore minor undulations, those are roads. Find clusters of right angles that repeat at similar sizes, those are platforms. Trace shallow trenches that tie elevations together, those are canals. Scan for mounds with smooth slopes and flattened tops, those are terraced civic cores. If the pattern persists over kilometers, you are not seeing natural drainage scars, you are seeing a designed landscape

What to do with rediscovered knowledge

The worst outcome is cargo cult replication, copying forms without copying mechanisms. The best outcome is translation. Take the Roman self-healing concept and build modern codes around it, for piers, sea walls, and low-maintenance bridges in corrosive environments. Pair Amazonian earthen urbanism with contemporary flood models and design amphibious neighborhoods that do not collapse in the first storm, that also support non-motorized mobility and biodiversity. Use acoustic insight to build courtrooms, classrooms, and clinics where voices are clear and stress is low, particularly for people with hearing differences. Treat pigments like Maya Blue as a materials science inspiration for non-toxic, long-lived coatings that cut maintenance cycles for public housing.

This is not about nostalgia or spectacle. It is a pragmatic research agenda hiding in plain sight. It makes budgets lighter, cities calmer, soils richer, and infrastructures slower to break. It also has cultural effects. It restores continuity. People are more willing to support conservation when the past is obviously useful, not only beautiful.

The responsible edge between wonder and evidence

Our book's title invites a strong claim that advanced civilizations existed long before recorded history. Here is the responsible version of that claim. Sophisticated, technically deep, environmentally tuned societies existed in many regions, some very early, some sustained for centuries, some organized as low-density urban mosaics rather than centralized stone metropolises. The Amazon case shows how easily such societies vanish from view when they build with mud and wood under a rainforest canopy. The acoustics cases show that empirically tuned spaces can formalize experience with measurable physical correlates. The materials cases show that "modern" breakthroughs often rediscover process wisdom that went missing for social reasons, not because it never worked. None of this requires a lost global superculture. All of it requires a serious revision of our mental timeline.

Where evidence is thin or absent, say so. Where new sensors open old landscapes, follow the data. And where an ancient solution beats a modern habit on durability or ecological fit, copy it with credit, optimize it with measurement, and teach it as if our grandchildren's budgets depend on it. They do.

Closing, with practical steps

If you are a builder, pilot self-healing lime mixes on non-critical structures and publish the monitoring data openly so code bodies can learn fast. If you are a planner, push for LIDAR surveys in your basin, then overlay hydrology, soils, and conservation priorities to guide both preservation and smart growth. If you are a farmer or extension worker in tropical belts, co-design biochar and compost protocols that respect local feedstocks and cuisines. If you are a curator or educator, add a small acoustic lab to your exhibit on prehistoric monuments and let visitors feel the difference between a dry room and a tuned one.

Most of all, treat the ancients as colleagues across time. They are not props for our myths; they are peers who solved hard problems with what they had. Our task is not to marvel, it is to learn, test, and translate.

Chapter 11

Rethinking Human History

The thesis is simple and uncomfortable: our standard story of civilization is too narrow, too linear, and too confident. When you hold Göbekli Tepe in one hand and the Antikythera Mechanism in the other, you are forced to ask whether human ingenuity has appeared in pulses rather than in a clean upward slope. The evidence hints at cycles: rise, complexity, overreach, correction, and rebirth. This is not a call to romanticize lost golden ages; it is a call to widen the frame so we can see the full pattern of human persistence.

Sanctuary & Science
Göbekli Tepe (c. 9600-8200 BCE) and the Antikythera Mechanism (1.d c. BCE)

Why our textbooks cling to a narrow version of civilization

Open a typical textbook, and the plot points are familiar: farming arrives in the Fertile Crescent, cities rise, writing follows, states consolidate, science and industry accelerate, and here we are. That outline is tidy and teachable, which is precisely why it lingers. The problem is not that it is false; the problem is that it is partial.

First, institutions favor clarity: syllabi, exams, and standardized curricula prefer sequences with beginnings and ends. A single timeline is easier to scale across classrooms than parallel streams that start, stop, and start again. The result is a linear narrative that compresses anomalies into footnotes.

Second, evidence from deep time is uneven. Stone, bone, and fired clay survive well; wood, fiber, and soft metals do not. A society that works wood with exquisite mastery, that sails on stitched hulls, that calculates with perishable devices, will vanish far more completely than a society that builds in dressed limestone. Preservation bias is not a conspiracy; it is a filter that amplifies some technologies while muting others.

Third, disciplinary silos create blind spots. Archaeologists know the contexts of sites, engineers know the loads stone can take, astronomers know celestial cycles, linguists study oral tradition, and computer scientists decode patterns. The most revealing signals sit at the intersections, yet academic incentives still reward depth within fields more than breadth across them.

Fourth, risk aversion keeps textbooks conservative. Claims that redraw maps or push dates earlier invite scrutiny, so they are accepted slowly. That caution is healthy in method, but when new findings accumulate in multiple lines, hesitation can become inertia.

Finally, there is a psychological comfort in progress stories. A clean ascent reassures us that history is a staircase and we are on the top step. Cycles complicate that comfort. They suggest that brilliance is not guaranteed, and that loss can be as real as gain.

What a wider frame looks like

When you bring Göbekli Tepe into focus, you see organized labor, monumental planning, sophisticated symbolism, and probable ritual astronomy at a time that was once assumed to be strictly proto-agrarian. When you study the Antikythera Mechanism, you see precise gear trains that encode cycles of the sun and moon, eclipse prediction, and calendrical coordination in a device that implies a tradition of mechanical design rather than an isolated genius. Between those anchors stretch dozens of cases where craft, math, and organization outpace the standard timeline for their context.

This does not prove a single worldwide lost civilization; it does prove that pockets of advanced capability have appeared earlier, more often, and in more places than a linear story makes room for. If we accept that, we must also accept that capability can be lost, then reinvented, then lost again.

The case for cycles of rise, collapse, and rebirth

Civilizations are ecological systems. They channel energy through networks of people, infrastructure, and information. As networks grow, they gain power through coordination, then face costs that grow faster than benefits: maintenance, administration, and defensive overhead. Add climate swings, disease, and trade shocks, and you get nonlinearity. That is where cycles begin.

How cycles form

1. **Innovation surge**: a stack of advances clusters in time, often across domains. Example patterns include improved food production, better transport, and new information systems. Labor reorganizes, elites mobilize surplus, monumental works appear, and symbolic systems codify authority.

2. **Complexity ramp**: coordination costs rise. Bureaucracies multiply, supply chains lengthen, and knowledge becomes specialized. The system becomes more capable, yet also more fragile, because losing any key node starts a cascade.

3. **External shocks**: climate variability, volcanic events, long droughts, sudden cooling, or floods. Sometimes the trigger is entirely social: over-expansion, internal conflict, unsustainable extraction.

4. **Break point**: networks desynchronize. Trade routes stutter, elite projects lose legitimacy, and local communities fall back to simpler arrangements that work with fewer assumptions about long-distance exchange.

5. **Cultural memory and seed banks**: skills do not vanish all at once. Techniques persist in guilds, households, ritual calendars, and stories. When energy returns, people draw from those reservoirs, often without knowing their full origins.

6. **Recombination and rebirth**: later societies rediscover and reassemble fragments into new stacks. The result may look like a fresh invention even when it carries faint echoes of prior knowledge.

Why "collapse" can be misleading

A collapse suggests a cliff. The reality is usually a slope with landings. Cities shrink, not vanish. Trade narrows to essential goods. Writing becomes rarer, yet oral law strengthens. Plumbing breaks in palaces while village irrigation persists. When the slope is steep and the landing low, later observers see a gap and misread it as an absence of capability rather than a reconfiguration.

What cycles do to timelines

If cycles are real, then firsts are less important than thresholds. Monumental stone architecture may be a threshold of coordination rather than a debut of intelligence. Complex astronomical models may appear whenever observational continuity meets practical need, such as agriculture, ritual calendars, or navigation. The key variable is not genius; it is network stability across generations. When that stability breaks, knowledge transmission attenuates.

Two anchors: Göbekli Tepe and the Antikythera Mechanism

Göbekli Tepe, the hill that rewrote prehistory

On a limestone ridge in southeastern Anatolia, circles of T-shaped pillars rise from the earth. The pillars are massive, expertly set in sockets, and carved with reliefs of foxes, snakes, boars, vultures, and abstract symbols. The site is layered, rebuilt, and ritually buried, which tells you two crucial things: the builders were not improvising, and they were thinking across generations.

The surprise is not simply that it is old; the surprise is that it is coordinated. You need quarrying teams, stone shapers, transport crews, site planners, and ritual specialists to sustain a project like that. You need food surpluses or well-organized feasts. You need a calendar that reliably tells people when to gather. None of this requires a city or wheat in fields; it requires social software that works at scale. That is the insight textbooks struggle to fit: people organized at high levels before sedentary urban life became the default.

Possible functions are debated: cult center, seasonal aggregation point, initiatory complex, sky watching platform, or all of the above at different phases. The carved menagerie is not random. It encodes a taxonomy that mattered to those who carved it. If the symbols track seasons or stars, that would be evidence of observing, counting, and predicting. Even if the imagery is primarily social or mythic, the planning logic remains advanced.

The Antikythera Mechanism, the bronze book of cycles

Recovered from a Hellenistic shipwreck, the corroded bronze looked like a lump. X-rays revealed gear trains, inscriptions, and dials. Reconstructed, it became a window into precision cognition: a device that models the motions of the heavens, tracks lunar phases with a subtle correction for the moon's variable speed, predicts eclipses, and coordinates calendars across Greek games and cities.

No one builds a device like that at the beginning of a tradition. The tolerances, the epicyclic logic, and the inscriptional clarity all point to a workshop culture where such problems are normal. You do not train artisans to cut that gear profile in one generation without prior steps in clocks, automata, or planetaria. That does not mean earlier devices survived; it means the mechanism you are holding is not an isolated spark.

What followed is its own lesson. The Roman world excelled at logistics and construction, yet prized different mechanical ends. The workshop lineage implied by the mechanism did not become the default basis of timekeeping. That was not because people forgot how to think; it was

What one device implies

A single complex artifact implies a scaffold of tacit knowledge, toolkits, apprenticeships, patrons, and problems worth solving. When the scaffold breaks, the artifact vanishes from production even if the idea survives in text or memory.

because patronage, demand, and institutional continuity shifted. Later, complex geared clocks reemerged in medieval Europe, a rebirth that looks like an invention, yet may have distant echoes of problems already solved.

Mainstream and heterodox, side by side

A responsible narrative holds two views at once. The mainstream view emphasizes gradual accumulation, local innovation, and convergent solutions. The heterodox view points to anomalies, earlier peaks, and cross-cultural patterning that suggest longer arcs of capability. The truth may be a braid of both.

Mainstream cautions: Extraordinary claims require consilient evidence, which means dates anchored in multiple methods, provenience tightly controlled, and mechanisms that explain transmission. Without those, speculation outruns data. Genuine frauds and sincere errors have occurred in the past, so skepticism is part of the toolkit.

Heterodox strengths: Outlier sites, precision workmanship in difficult contexts, and pattern echoes in myths and alignments deserve patient study. Repeated appearance of complex ideas in widely separated cultures may reflect convergent solutions to universal problems, or it may signal deep time sharing along migration and trade corridors that we have not fully mapped.

Holding both views produces better work. The standard narrative becomes flexible where the data insist; the speculative narrative becomes disciplined where the data resist.

Case Study: Cross-cultural myths as coded history

Myths are not minutes from a council meeting; they are cultural memory shaped by performance, repetition, and meaning. Yet they carry payloads of information. When the same motif appears across far-separated peoples, you ask what mechanism could achieve that: diffusion across long trade networks, deep ancestry before groups separated, or convergence because people everywhere face the same sky, sea, animals, and hazards.

Floods, fires, and falling skies

Flood stories are nearly universal. The details vary: a divine decision, a warning to a single family, a boat or basket, animals preserved, waters that cover the land, a mountain landing, a covenant sign. In some versions, the earth is tilted or the sky descends; in others, the sea bursts its bounds. If you strip away names and focus on functions, you get a memory of sudden inundation and survival planning. That can code for river megafloods, coastal storm surges, glacial lake outbursts, or tsunamis after quakes or submarine slides. Oral tradition can hold the outline of such events for long periods when they are retold at rites of passage, harvests, and memorials.

Fire from the sky is another wide motif. It can be meteors, airburst events, or volcanic ash that darkens daylight. Communities do not need astrophysics to remember that red stones fell with noise, that fields burned without visible flame, or that ash made noon dim. Over time, the story takes moral shape, yet the physical cues remain precise enough to be testable when mapped to local geology.

The motif of a lost island or sunken city often couples with a flood, with moral or political lessons. The test, again, is not whether every story is literal; the test is whether clusters of stories line up with zones of rapid sea level rise on once habitable coastal plains now on the continental shelf. If they do, then myth has coded real geography into narrative.

Sky knowledge and precision hints

Myths do more than warn. They schedule. Naming constellations, tying god stories to star risings and settings, and embedding seasonal work in sky signals are practical. Over centuries, storytellers have noticed that the timing drifts. That drift is due to the precession of the equinoxes, a slow wobble of Earth's axis. You do not need equations to track drift; you need patient sky watching across generations and a culture that cares about calibration. When tales note that a sacred star no longer rises where it used to, you are hearing observational astronomy expressed as religion. When symbol sets match animal constellations with seasonal tasks, you are seeing calendars with teeth.

This does not prove advanced precessional theory in deep prehistory, it does prove that people kept score, compared grandparent sky to grandchild sky, and encoded that in ways that survive long after temple walls fall.

Why capability can hide in plain sight

We tend to rank societies by monuments, then by metals, then by manuscripts. That ladder misses three factors that often matter more: networks, maintenance, and interface.

1. **Networks:** Expertise can concentrate in guilds serving seafaring, pilgrimage, or ritual centers. If the node disappears, the expertise goes quiet, not extinct.

2. **Maintenance:** Complex systems fail silently when spare parts and calibration routines vanish. A device without service falls to the level of scrap in a single generation.

3. **Interface:** Some knowledge travels in songs, dances, and diagrams in sand. Outsiders may not notice that a chant

encodes a star path, or that a decorative border ticks a lunar count, or that a story game is an algorithm for resource rotation.

A tour of signal cases that widen the frame

Megalithic engineering and organization

Building in multi-ton blocks is not a brute force contest; it is a planning problem. You need quarries sited to select rock with the right bedding planes, roads or sled paths prepared in seasonal windows, rope and lever systems proportioned to the load, and teams trained to read stone. Accuracy in jointing and alignment comes from patient iteration, simple tools used expertly, and social time that runs on ritual calendars, which ensure crews return on schedule.

The key lesson is that technique stacks are portable across materials. Once you have a culture of measurement and verification, you can apply it to stone, timber, and even earthworks with equal rigor. When you see consistent angular alignments and repeatable module sizes across sites, you are likely looking at a shared design language.

Early seafaring as a knowledge multiplier

Open water voyages force you to integrate star knowledge, wave reading, wind seasons, and provisioning. Small island colonizations imply deliberate navigation, not accidental drift. When people mastered these routines, they knitted coasts into information webs. Ideas ride with people. Motifs in art, useful plants, shell bead standards, and even calendar schemas can move along these blue corridors. The sea preserves little; the tradition preserves a lot.

Calendars hidden in plain sight

In multiple cultures, notches, cords, or painted tally marks match lunar months, agricultural tasks, and festivals. When those marks are also correct for drift, or tie lunar and solar cycles with intercalations, you are looking at thinking with feedback. Over time, that grows into devices and tables. Whether written in bark, knotted into fiber, or cast in bronze, the underlying mind is the same: observe, record, model, predict, and adjust.

Rethinking how knowledge moves

The image of ideas leaping oceans in a single bound is tempting and often wrong. Transmission works best along stepping stones: valleys, coasts, oases, and markets. Caravans carry more than goods; they carry techniques, scripts, and stories. Mariners carry more than cargo; they carry star paths and port protocols. When those routes falter, the flow thins. When routes revive, so does exchange.

That is why some seemingly independent inventions can in fact be cousins. A gear is a simple idea once you have lathes, gauges, and the habit of tolerances. The leap from water lifting screws to astronomical calculators is not magic; it is patronage plus patience in workshops that solve one precise problem after another until the solution space expands.

What this means for education and public understanding

If we keep teaching a single staircase, students will keep missing the landings and ramps. A better curriculum would treat human history as a braided river, not a pipe. It would teach method first: how to weigh claims, how to cross-check dates, how to distinguish what the ground says from what we wish it said. It would show how underwater archaeology changes the map of early coasts, how paleoclimate adds context, and how genetics fills migration corridors without replacing cultural history.

A better museum label would say: "Here is what is certain, here is what is probable, here is what is proposed, and here is what would change our minds." That is not hedging, that is honesty.

How cycles change our sense of ourselves

The linear story says we are the culmination. The cyclical story says we are at a current crest. Those are not the same thing. A crest is impressive, yet contingent. It depends on many waves that rose and fell before it. That shift matters because it breeds humility and care. If capability can slip, then stewardship of knowledge becomes an ethical duty, not just a curiosity.

Consider Göbekli Tepe again. Its planners thought in centuries and buried their own work with intention. Consider the workshop behind the Antikythera Mechanism. Its makers assumed clients would continue to value calibrated models of the sky. Both assumptions failed in time. The lesson is not despair, it is continuity by design: build institutions that expect interruptions and write playbooks for relaunch.

A reconciliation that respects both caution and wonder

We do not need to choose between sobriety and surprise. The sober view guards the gates against wishful thinking. The surprised view keeps us looking at the horizon. In practice, the best work proceeds like this: treat anomalies as opportunities to refine models; upgrade models when clusters of anomalies survive testing; keep an open slot on the shelf for the next puzzle that will not fit.

That, in the end, is what "advanced" really means: not a fixed level, but a culture able to learn, unlearn, and relearn. When you recognize that pattern, you stop asking whether a single ancient global civilization existed and start asking where, when, and how often human communities reached high capability, then carried it forward or fumbled it. You also start asking what we are doing now that will look like a fumble to descendants.

A method walk-through: side-by-side reading of two puzzles

Puzzle one: a monument aligned with stars

Observation: a set of standing stones frames a sunrise on a specific day.

Mainstream reading: agricultural scheduling, ritual marking of seasonal change, inter-community coordination.

Heterodox addition: precessional drift implies long-term observation and correction protocols that may encode more than a simple marking.

Test path: survey for sightlines, check horizon profile, simulate sky across plausible dates, look for corrective construction phases, and search for associated tally artifacts.

Outcome: If the phases track drift, you have evidence of feedback in calendrical practice, which is a clear marker of an advanced timekeeping culture for that era.

Puzzle two: a mechanism fragment with teeth

Observation: a corroded plate with gear teeth and faint inscriptions.

Mainstream reading: part of a calendrical or display device, likely elite-owned, requires precision metalwork and standard gauges.

Heterodox addition: the inscriptional program hints at functions beyond display, such as predictive corrections and multi-calendar coordination.

Test path: micro CT or equivalent imaging, tooth count reconstruction, inscription recovery with raking light and multispectral photography, replication of gear trains in modern materials to verify function space.

Outcome: if the function matches predictions and inscriptions name multiple cycles with corrections, you have a strong case for a mature branch of applied astronomy and mechanics rather than a curiosity.

Ethical stakes: what we owe to the dead and the unborn

There is dignity in giving the past its due breadth. People who carved pillars on windswept ridges and makers who cut fine gears in cramped workshops deserve to be seen not as exceptions, but as expressions of a durable human capacity. Widening the frame also binds us to the future. If knowledge is cyclical, then we are custodians, not owners. Our task is to compress as many hard-won methods into resilient channels as we can, so that when interruptions come, restart is easier.

That means budgeting for archives, training generalists who can bridge fields, and celebrating maintainers alongside inventors. It means teaching students to love problems more than answers. It means treating the sea floor and the desert as libraries whose catalogs we are still writing.

From doubt to discipline: how to proceed from here

1. **Underwater coastlines:** Push survey and excavation on submerged shelves that were dry during lower sea levels. Expect to find habitations, fisheries, and possibly ritual sites that explain why flood stories fixate on sudden loss.

2. **High-resolution climate backdrops:** Pair each cultural horizon with precise climate curves. When people adjust calendars, move settlements, or change their diet, ask what the sky and sea were doing.

3. **Device lineage mapping:** Treat the Antikythera Mechanism as a node in a missing network. Look for textual descriptions of devices, workshop marks on unrelated bronzes that imply gear cutting capability, and tool marks on stone that betray machine-like regularity.

4. **Ritual as registry:** Analyze ceremonies for embedded counts. Steps, offerings, chants, and dance figures often encode cycles. Cross-reference these with observable astronomical events to reconstruct community timekeeping.

5. **Apprenticeship archaeology:** Search for training spaces: practice slabs with half-cut lines, miscast gears, broken bow drills, and teaching diagrams. These reveal the living pipeline more than perfect masterpieces do.

Closing the loop: what Göbekli Tepe and the Antikythera Mechanism tell us together

One stands at the dawn of settled ritual, the other at the height of a specific mechanical craft. Both say the same quiet thing: people, given time, feedback, and purpose, will build systems that reach beyond immediate subsistence. They will count more carefully than necessary, align more precisely than required, and encode meaning in durable forms. Sometimes those systems endure; sometimes they fall into the earth or the sea and wait for us to hear them again.

The standard story, trimmed for classrooms, misses that heartbeat. The cyclical story hears it, not as mysticism, but as a pattern. Rise, complexity, shock, reconfiguration, renewal. If we write history that way, we honor the ingenuity of ancestors and prepare successors to face interruptions without panic. We also learn to see anomalies not as threats, but as invitations.

Chapter 12

Listening to the Echoes

The stones that rise from the plateau at Göbekli Tepe, the green patina spreading across the Antikythera Mechanism's bronze gears, the deliberately flooded chambers under forgotten harbors, the precise astronomical alignments etched into megalithic corridors, these are not just artifacts; they are signals. They tell us that the past was not empty; it was busy. It was busy with experiments in social organization, with difficult logistics, with sky watching, with memory storage and transmission, with engineering choices made under hard constraints. When we listen properly, those signals say something useful about our future. They also challenge a comfortable assumption, the belief that we are the first truly advanced civilization. The honest answer is more nuanced: we are the first global, fossil-fuel-intensive, electronically networked civilization on record, yet we might not be the first to achieve pockets of startling sophistication, and we might not be the last. That distinction matters for how we plan, how we store knowledge, and how we measure our real progress.

Setting the terms clearly

Before going deeper, let us define a few working terms, so the discussion stays focused and fair.

An **advanced civilization**, in this chapter, means a society that can coordinate complex projects across thousands of people, sustain specialized labor for generations, generate surplus energy beyond subsistence, encode and preserve knowledge at scale, and consciously measure itself against celestial cycles or deep time. It does not require microchips. It does require systems thinking, planning horizons longer than a lifetime, and mastery of logistics and materials.

A **technological signature** is any durable, measurable footprint that indicates systematic knowledge of nature put to repeatable use. Aligning a megalithic complex to solar or lunar standstills counts. Mass producing precision stone blocks with standardized joint counts. Casting bronze with controlled alloy ratios counts. Building a mechanical astronomical computer to track cycle counts. These signatures are not limited to factories and semiconductors.

A **civilizational blind spot** is a domain where a society performs brilliantly, but leaves little or misleading residue for future archaeologists to find. Organic media, timber architecture, coastal cities that later drown or erode, and distributed know-how held in guilds rather than in public inscriptions are all classic blind spots.

With these terms in place, we can listen to the echoes with fewer distractions and fewer straw men.

What these mysteries tell us about our own future

The headline lesson is simple and sobering: complexity is perishable. That does not mean complexity always collapses; it means complexity must be actively maintained. When we study ancient anomalies and achievements with generosity and rigor, we see three recurring truths that should shape our future decisions: knowledge decays without deliberate redundancy, energy regimes determine what is buildable and maintainable, and memory must survive through format shifts and environmental shocks.

Knowledge decays without redundancy

Göbekli Tepe shows coordinated construction, long planning, food surplus sufficient to feed specialists who carved and erected towering pillars, and symbol systems that meant enough to motivate centuries of work. The site was later deliberately buried. Whether the burial was ritual, protective, or part of a planned decommissioning, the lesson for us is this: cultural memory can be intentionally archived, and it can also be intentionally hidden. Hiding is not preservation unless the future knows where and how to look. Today, our knowledge sits on fragile stacks of code, file formats, and servers that expect uninterrupted energy and steady institutional continuity. The ancient builders force us to ask a tough question: if we turned off the power for a hundred years, how much of our science would be recoverable from physical inscriptions, durable artifacts, and human memory practices alone?

Why redundancy beats brilliance

Redundancy is not waste, it is strategy. A single medium, a single archive, or a single institutional host invites erasure by accident or by design. Copying knowledge into different materials, different languages, and different regions multiplies the chance that at least one copy survives a flood, a fire, a war, or a political purge. That is as true for climate data and vaccine protocols as it is for epics and law codes.

Why redundancy beats brilliance

Redundancy is not waste; it is a strategy. A single medium, a single archive, or a single institutional host invites erasure by accident or by design. Copying knowledge into different materials, different languages, and different regions multiplies the chance that at least one copy survives a flood, a fire, a war, or a political purge. That is as true for climate data and vaccine protocols as it is for epics and law codes.

Three Archives of One Knowledge

Stone Inscription (dry cave)	Acid-free Print Volumes (sealed shelf)	Micro-etched Nickel (under glass)

Energy regimes decide what is possible and what lasts.

The Antikythera Mechanism is the clearest counterexample to the idea that high precision must wait for steam engines or fossil fuels. Craftspeople used hand tools, alloys, and mathematical insight to create a portable, gear-based model of the heavens. That tells us two things about the future. First, high precision is not the same as high energy. Second, a civilization's toolkit can be narrow but deep. Depth in a chosen toolkit produces results that look magical to outsiders. We, in turn, should not assume that only one energy pathway, our modern fossil-to-electrons chain, can support advanced capability. Solar thermal with clever mechanics, tidal flows with flywheels, biological energy organized at scale, and low-tech high-skill approaches can carry surprising loads if designed with longevity in mind.

Memory must cross formats and shocks.

Ancient builders expressed memory in stone, sky-aligned corridors, and ritual calendars. We express memory through cloud backups, which is a metaphor that hides a simple fact: the cloud is just someone else's computer on a power-hungry rack. If we want our descendants to remember orbital mechanics, material science, and public health, we must bridge formats. That means a layered approach: living traditions that practice knowledge in communities, analog summaries encoded in

---

Future-proofing essentials

1. A one-page analog summary for each vital domain, with diagrams and minimal language.
2. A robust analog core library stored in dry, cool, geopolitically diverse sites.
3. Open formats with public documentation, plus periodic migration schedules.
4. Community-level apprenticeships that embody the skills behind the text.

---

durable media, and digital archives with open standards.

Complexity thrives on institutional trust.

Ancient projects that spanned generations, from megalithic corridors to large irrigation fields, required social technologies that are harder to excavate than stone. Trust, credit, reputation, conflict mediation, and status management were as essential as chisels. Our future, therefore, depends on social protocols that can be audited, repaired, and transmitted as easily as technical know-how. This is not a sentimental point. It is an engineering constraint. Logistics and morale determine whether the quarry keeps sending blocks on time.

Are we the first advanced civilization, or one of many

This is the live wire. The phrase "advanced civilization" carries modern images of satellites and silicon. If we define it that narrowly, then yes, we are first on record. If we define it by capability rather than substrate, the answer opens up. The archaeological and geological records show repeated patterns of regional sophistication, sudden disruptions, partial recoveries, and long silences. What follows is a clear, balanced walk-through of the strongest arguments on both sides, so you can weigh them without drama.

The mainstream case for "first on record"

1. **Energy density and scope:** Only the modern world exhibits global energy capture at levels sufficient to sustain billions of people in cities with continuous electric networks, deep supply chains across continents, and spaceflight. Earlier societies display impressive regional feats, yet nothing points to a planet-spanning industrial system.

2. **Materials and residues:** Industrial modernity leaves distinct waste streams, such as synthetic polymers, long-chain organics, fly ash layers, nitrogen and carbon isotopic anomalies, and radionuclide traces. These are measurable, and they cluster in the most recent strata. Deeper layers contain metallurgical residues and mine tailings, but not the chemical fingerprints of modern high-throughput industry.

3. **Cumulative written records:** From clay tablets to codices to printed books, the textual chain of custody from early states to the present is partial yet visible. That continuity supports the claim that there was no large prior wave of world-spanning industry that then disappeared without a coherent textual memory.

4. **Population genetics and domesticates:** The distribution of domesticated plants and animals, and the genetic signatures of population expansions, align with a human story of gradual intensification. Nothing in the data requires a prior global industrial phase.

These points are strong. They are also framed against a specific image of "advance," one that emphasizes engines and mass chemistry. There is another lens.

The heterodox case for "one of many"

No responsible researcher claims a hidden global industrial civilization without evidence. What heterodox scholars and careful amateurs do claim is this: when you consider preservation biases, coastal loss, and the fragility of organic technology, it is plausible that multiple societies achieved higher peaks of organization and knowledge than our usual timelines imply. The argument has four pillars.

1. **Preservation bias and the coastal sieve:** Sea levels have risen since the last glacial maximum by well over a hundred meters. Any coastal urban belt built during lower sea levels would now be underwater or eroded. Since early complex societies exploited coasts and river deltas, a large share of high-value sites lie where we sample. This is not a conspiracy; it is a sampling problem. It means caution about drawing strong negative conclusions from a noisy dataset.

2. **Blind spots in organic tech:** A civilization that distributes know-how through oral guilds, uses timber, fiber, and resins, and relies on mechanical computation or biological energy can achieve remarkable effectiveness and still leave little behind. If such a society were disrupted by flood, disease, or migration, it might leave only small pockets of durable artifacts. We should not equate sparse residue with low capability.

3. **Evidence of precision without engines:** High-tolerance stonework, surveyed alignments to astronomical events, long-distance trade with standardized weights, and mechanical devices like geared calculators reveal a precision culture. Precision is a habit as much as a tool. It tends to emerge where social incentives reward repeatable, verifiable outcomes. That habit can lift performance across domains.

4. **Cultural memory as a noisy instrument:** Myths and calendars can remember events, yet they compress, dramatize, and blend. Firestorms become dragons, tsunamis become divine walls of water, sky events become omens. When multiple independent traditions converge on similar motifs, such as a rapid inundation or a cold shock, we should listen. Not as proof, but as prompts to look at where geology and archaeology can test.

These heterodox points do not overthrow the mainstream case. They add humility and curiosity. They say we do not yet know the upper bound of what earlier societies achieved in specific niches, especially where the excavation odds are poor.

The scale spectrum, not a binary

It helps to replace the binary question with a spectrum. On one end sits **craft civilization**, a society with deep expertise in limited toolsets, high social coordination, and durable cultural memory. On the other end sits **machine civilization**, a society with high energy throughput, automated production, planet-scale logistics, and digital memory. Many ancient societies reached the craft civilization zone. We occupy the machine civilization zone. The spectrum reminds us that capability is multidimensional. It also suggests a strategy: craft skills endure shocks better than machine dependencies, while machines multiply reach when energy is cheap and stable. The wise path blends both.

Patterns behind the peaks and breaks

If we listen carefully to the echoes from many regions, we hear recurring patterns: long learning curves, sudden accelerations, social friction points, and recurrent vulnerabilities. Understanding those patterns is the practical payoff, because they tell us where to invest for longevity.

The long apprenticeship

Grand projects generally started small. Trial stones, rough alignments, misfits, and later corrections appear at many sites when layers are documented carefully. This rebuts the view that complex structures appeared fully formed. Instead, builders used iterative design. Our future benefits from that same rhythm: prototype, test, review, revise, never assume the first elegant idea is the right one, and always capture the lessons learned in a format that novices can digest.

The acceleration phase

Once a coordination method proves itself, growth can be rapid. A trusted token system, an apprenticeship network, or a ritual calendar that aligns labor with seasonal windows can convert scattered efforts into a steady flow. The real mechanism of acceleration is not just tools. It is predictability. When every crew trusts that every other crew will do its part on time, scale follows.

Social friction points

Every complex system generates disputes over credit, access, and burden sharing. Many failures are social rather than technical. Rotating leadership, transparent tallies, and prestige awarded for maintenance work can calm friction. Our future needs governance that rewards stewards, not only founders.

Recurrent vulnerabilities

Four hazards show up repeatedly: coastal flooding and erosion, supply chain fragility across difficult terrain, elite predation on provisioning systems, and knowledge trapped in one language or sect. None of these is mysterious. They are practical. The mitigation playbook is also practical: site diversity, modular storage, transparent provisioning, multilingual summaries, and shared custody of critical knowledge across rival groups.

The future, seen through the oldest problems

When we look ahead, we tend to imagine brand new problems. Often, the oldest problems are still the ones that matter. Here is what the ancient echoes suggest about the real levers of our future.

Build archives as if no battery will be found.

Digital storage is rich yet brittle. We should act as if every crucial body of knowledge might need to be restarted by people with no access to our grids, who nevertheless have sharp minds and patient hands. That means three layers of preservation, not one. A body of knowledge should exist as a practiced craft, as a durable analog reference, and as an open digital repository. Only the triple layer creates real security.

Practical Resilience: Sun, Sanitation, and Storage

Design for repair, not only performance

The past is full of examples where performance was excellent but maintainability was poor. Our future must prefer architectures where every component can be replaced by hand with basic tools, where functions degrade gracefully rather than catastrophically, and where field guides assume that the repairer may have limited training.

Favor energy modesty with precision.

Precision is a mindset that can survive energy scarcity. In a world of supply chain shocks and climate disruptions, tools and processes that achieve precision with low energy input will carry communities through rough years. That does not mean rejecting high-energy tools. It means never making precision hostage to them.

Build city memory into the ground.

A city should teach you how to run it by walking through it. Wayfinding should reveal evacuation routes and resource caches.

Public squares should display analog panels that explain water distribution, power routing options, and contacts for neighborhood response. The ancient habit of placing knowledge in the built environment is still powerful. It bypasses literacy gaps and device failures.

Treat attention as a scarce mineral.

Coordination fails when attention is noisy or exhausted. The clearest lesson from long, multi-generation projects is that ceremonial cycles doubled as attention management systems. They mobilized people at the right time, set expectations, and reduced confusion. We should design modern equivalents that are secular, transparent, and evidence-based, such as seasonal maintenance festivals where the prestige goes to crews who service the unglamorous assets, like drainage and pumps.

Testing the "many civilizations" hypothesis without fantasies

Curiosity is good. So is discipline. If we want to assess whether we are one of many advanced civilizations in a deep historical sense, we need testable proposals and fieldwork that does not presuppose its conclusion. Here are sober, practical approaches.

Go to the right places.

Search for drowned continental shelves, paleo-coastlines, and river mouths that were dry and habitable during lower sea stands. Use side-scan sonar, sub-bottom profiling, and targeted coring to look for cultural layers. If we do not look, we should stop making strong claims in any direction. Looking is the honest path.

Hunt for the right signals

We should not expect skyscrapers on the sea floor. We should look for anthropogenic sediments, unusual concentrations of certain metals or slags, cut or jointed stones, harbor residues, geometrically regular foundations, and gardens or fields with nonrandom patterns of soil modification. We should expect partial, weathered fragments, and then we should connect them into a coherent story only with patient cross-checks.

Seek tool marks and metrology.

Ancient workmanship often reveals itself through tool signatures and measurement systems. Periodic spacing, repeated tolerances, and consistent angles hint at standardized training and reference tools. Metrology is civilization's private fingerprint. When we find it, we are close to the people who made it.

Use geology as an ally, not an adversary.

Rapid climate swings, volcanic events, and climatic oscillations leave clear stratigraphic markers. If a site, artifact, or myth points to a disruption, look for the geological marker that matches its time window. Aligning cultural and geological clocks produces a tighter, more credible narrative, whether the result supports mainstream expectations or challenges them.

The moral of the Antikythera, the lesson of Göbekli

Two sites, two messages. The mechanical computer at sea and the buried sanctuary on land speak across time in complementary voices.

From the Antikythera device, we learn that precision is an attitude before it is a machine. An attitude can be taught, practiced, and passed on even when resources are humble. If we want our descendants to inherit a civilization worth the effort, we must cultivate the attitude that celebrates accurate measurement, careful assembly, and honest error correction.

From Göbekli Tepe, we learn that humans will give decades to shared symbols and will feed specialists when the story compels them. Meaning is leverage. If meaning points to works that improve water, soil, health, and memory, meaning becomes a tool of resilience. If meaning is captured by those who value status over stewardship, meaning becomes a solvent that dissolves the commons.

The humility clause

We close with humility. The temptation to judge the past by the yardsticks of the present is strong. When we do that, we shrink the range of possible answers. A fair reading of the evidence says this: earlier societies achieved deep competence, wide coordination, and memorable beauty, often with low energy budgets and durable techniques. They also suffered reversals that erased libraries, drowned coasts, and scattered workshops. We should therefore speak about our status carefully.

We are first at a specific combination of scale, energy, and circuitry. We are not first at building precise instruments, not first at aligning time with stone, not first at coordinating complex tasks across many crews, and not first at designing social rituals that organize labor over long horizons. If we insist on one yardstick, we score a decisive first. If we adopt a richer rubric, we find company, and we learn more.

That honesty does not diminish our achievements. It clarifies our task. Our job is not to congratulate ourselves for uniqueness; it is to make ourselves good ancestors.

Listening forward

Listening to echoes is not a retreat into nostalgia. It is a forward-looking discipline. When we sift the old signals, we learn how to design cities that remember how to run themselves, how to preserve knowledge for those we will never meet, how to train hands and minds to achieve precision without expensive energy, and how to reward the stewards who keep water flowing and drains clear. We learn to make meaning pull in the direction of maintenance, not only monuments.

We also learn to respect the experiment. Civilizations are experiments in how to turn energy and attention into lasting value. Some experiments succeed for centuries, then drift, then break. Others burn bright and short. We do not control all variables, yet we control more than we admit. The most controllable variable is our attitude toward memory and repair.

Final counsel from the echoes

If the pillars and the gears could speak, they would probably skip the flattery and offer three pieces of counsel.

First, audit your dependencies. Write them down. Energy sources, spare parts, skilled labor, raw materials, and legal permissions. Anything you cannot replace or bypass within a season is a risk. Reduce that list each year.

Second, favor legible systems. If newcomers cannot figure out how your water plant or your archive works by reading the labels and diagrams on site, you are courting amnesia.

Third, celebrate the boring work. Civilization survives not because someone invented a marvelous device, but because crews cleaned filters, patched roofs, dredged canals, updated manuals, and trained replacements. Honor them in public, not just in private memos.

A calm answer to the big question

Are we the first advanced civilization, or one of many? The honest answer is layered.

At the level of the global electrified industry, we are first on record. At the level of durable precision, long-horizon planning, and complex coordination, we have predecessors who, within their energy and material regimes, reached impressive heights. Those predecessors are not rivals. They are collaborators across time. Their lessons are not warnings alone. They are instructions.

Our future, if it is to be long, will look less like a sustained fireworks show and more like a well-run workshop and a well-tended watershed, precise in its habits, modest in its energy appetite, generous in its copying of knowledge, and clever in its recruitment of meaning for maintenance. That is not a retreat. It is a mature ambition. It is how a civilization becomes hard to erase.

Listening to the echoes changes how we hear ourselves. We stop asking only whether the past had engines, and we start asking whether it had wisdom about maintenance, memory, and meaning. Then we look at our cities and measure ourselves by the same criteria. When we do, a simple path appears. Build things that can be repaired by hand. Teach skills as if batteries may fail. Inscribe the critical summaries into the buildings themselves. Keep multiple copies in different places and different tongues. Reward the custodians. Align work with seasonal cycles that people can feel in their bones.

That is how you honor the pillars on the plateau and the gears in the sea. That is how you become not just first at something, but durable at everything that matters. That is how your descendants will one day listen to your echoes and say, they thought ahead, they cared for those they would never meet, they left us instructions, and they made it easy to keep going.

Bonus Section:

Ancient Echoes Workbook

A practical companion to Ancient Echoes: From Göbekli Tepe to the Antikythera Mechanism

Y ou are not here to passively read; you are here to investigate. Use this workbook like field gear: write in it, sketch in it, argue in the margins, and leave space for the next round of insight. The pages below are deliberately straightforward, with wide spaces for answers and repeatable tasks you can run on your own.

How to use this workbook

1. **Timeline:** build your running chronology from 10,000 BCE onward. Each entry gives you a concise starter, then you fill in the specifics you care about.

2. **Reflection prompts:** pressure test your beliefs, then rewrite them in plain language.

3. **Practical exercises:** track sky events, reconstruct calendar logic, and test alignments with simple tools.

4. **Further resources:** find archives and communities, and filter signal from noise with a credibility checklist.

Throughout, you will see short notes that anchor a prompt in the core ideas of the book, so your answers stay coherent. Examples include Göbekli Tepe as a coordination signal near the end of the last ice age, the Antikythera Mechanism as precision thinking in bronze, and archaeoacoustics that turn stone rooms into instruments.

Part A: Timeline of Artifacts and Anomalies from 10,000 BCE Onward

Goal: create a living chronology of sites, devices, and material surprises that matter to your thesis. Keep the entries crisp and testable: what it is, where it is, why it matters, what questions you still have.

Instructions

For each entry:

- Title the artifact or site.

- Add a rough date range and location.

- Summarize why it matters in two or three sentences.

- Record the mainstream reading in one or two sentences.

- Record any competing or heterodox reading you find persuasive in one or two sentences.

- Write your next action: a paper to find, a measurement to replicate, or a local museum to contact.

- Sketch the key geometry, mechanism, or layout.

Leave room to revise, since your view should sharpen as you work across the book.

10,000 to 9000 BCE: Göbekli Tepe, Southeastern Anatolia

Starter context: You are dealing with T-shaped pillars, reliefs, sockets, rebuilds, and evidence of deliberate burial. The headline is not only about age, but it is also about coordination and planning before settled urban life became dominant.

- **Title:**

  _____

- Date range and location:
  _____

- Why it matters:

_____

_____

_____

_____

_____

_____

_____

_____

- Mainstream reading you will test:

_____

- Alternative reading you will test:

_____

- Next action:

_____

- Sketch box, plan, and section:
  [Space for drawing]

_____

_____

_____

_____

Notes:

_____

_____

_____

_____

_____

_____

_____

_____

4000 to 3000 BCE: Hal Saflieni Hypogeum, Malta

Starter context: measured resonances around 70 hertz and 110 to 114 hertz in the so-called Oracle Room, a response that sits in a baritone's range, and subjective reports of a body felt bloom. Treat this as a designed experience, not mysticism.

- Title:

_____

- Date   range   and   location:

  _____

- Why it matters:

  _____

  _____

  _____

  _____

  _____

- Mainstream reading you will test:

  _____

- Alternative reading you will test:

  _____

Next action, measurement plan:

Bring a small speaker, a tone generator from 60 to 300 hertz, and a phone RTA app. Map loud zones at 70, 110 to 114 hertz.

- Sketch box, plan view with hot spots:
  [Space for drawing]

  _____

  _____

  _____

  _____

_____

_____

_____

_____

a) 3200 BCE: Newgrange and Passage Tomb Tradition, Ireland

Starter context: repeated low-frequency room modes near 110 hertz in corbelled stone chambers, the kind of pitch that human voices can sustain.

- Title:

  _____

- Date   range   and   location:

  _____

- Why it matters:

  _____

- Mainstream reading you will test:

  _____

- Alternative reading you will test:

  _____

- Next action:

  _____

- Sketch box, section with corbelled vault:
  [Space for drawing]

_____

_____

_____

_____

_____

_____

_____

_____

b) 3000 to 2000 BCE: Stonehenge, Southern Britain

Starter context: scale model tests show sound inside the ring is measurably enhanced and more coherent than outside, which matters for ritual and coordination.

- Title:

_____

- Date   range   and   location:

_____

- Why it matters:

_____

_____

_____

_____

- Mainstream reading you will test:

_____

_____

_____

_____

Alternative reading you will test:

_____

_____

_____

_____

- Next action, model idea:

Build a small ring with stones or blocks and clap tests inside versus outside, log decay time with a phone app.

- Sketch box, plan, and ring densities:
  [Space for drawing]

_____

_____

_____

_____

_____

_____

c) 1200 to 500 BCE: Chavín de Huántar, Peru

Starter context: instrument architecture duet with pututu conch trumpets and stone galleries that mask direction and project tones, a case where instruments and space clearly cooperate.

- Title:

  _____

- Date   range   and   location:

  _____

- Why it matters:

  _____

  _____

  _____

  _____

- Mainstream reading you will test:

  _____

  _____

  _____

  _____

- Alternative reading you will test:

_____

_____

_____

_____

- **Next action:**

Sketch the gallery network, mark suspected source points, and plan a beat frequency test with two-tone sources.

- **Sketch box, gallery plan with arrows:**
  [Space for drawing]

_____

_____

_____

_____

_____

_____

_____

_____

_____

_____

_____

_____

_____

_____

_____

_____

_____

_____

_____

_____

d) 2nd to 1st century BCE: The Antikythera Mechanism, Aegean

Starter context: a hand-cranked astronomical computer that models the Sun and Moon against the zodiac, includes a clever correction for the Moon's uneven speed, predicts eclipse seasons, and ties civic calendars to cycles.

- Title:

  _____

- Date range and location:

  _____

- Why it matters:

_____

_____

_____

_____

_____

Mainstream reading you will test:

_____

_____

_____

_____

Alternative reading you will test:

_____

_____

_____

_____

Next action: build a paper dial:

Construct a front dial with a zodiac and calendar, then a back spiral for a 19-year cycle. See exercises in Part C.

- **Sketch box, front and back faces:**
- [Space for drawing]

_____

_____

_____

_____

_____

_____

_____

e) 1st century CE onward: The Memnon "voice," Egypt

Starter context: Dawn sounds once linked to fissures and heat in quartzite at the Colossi of Memnon, likely a physical phenomenon later silenced by repair. Use it as a reminder that stones can be instruments by accident and by design.

- Title:

  _____

- Date   range   and   location:

  _____

- Why it matters:

_____

_____

_____

_____

_____

_____

_____

_____

- Mainstream reading you will test:

_____

_____

_____

_____

_____

_____

- Alternative reading you will test:

_____

Next action:

_____

_____

Sketch box, statue detail, and fissure paths:
[Space for drawing]

_____

_____

_____

_____

_____

_____

_____

f) 1st millennium BCE to 1st millennium CE: Roman Maritime Concrete

Starter context: lime plus volcanic ash systems that, in sea environments, grow protective minerals, bridge pores, and self-heal microcracks over time, a durability profile modern mixes rarely match in salt water. Use this as your "materials maturity" case.

- Title:

  _____

- Date   range   and   location:

  _____

- Why it matters:

_____

_____

Mainstream reading you will test:

_____

_____

_____

_____

- Alternative reading you will test:

_____

_____

- Next action:

_____

_____

_____

_____

_____

- Sketch box, core sample with needles and lime clasts: [Space for drawing]

_____

_____

_____

_____

g) 200 BCE to 1700 CE, with modern revivals: Crucible Steels and "Damascus" Patterns

Starter context: watered patterns that originate either from layered assembly or from carbide networks in crucible steels, with mechanical consequences for edge retention and toughness. Distinguish routes, then judge blades by microstructure and performance, not by name alone.

- Title:

- Date   range   and   location:

- Why it matters:

- Mainstream reading you will test:

- Alternative reading you will test:

- Next action:

_____

- Sketch box, microstructure bands versus layers:
  [Space for drawing]

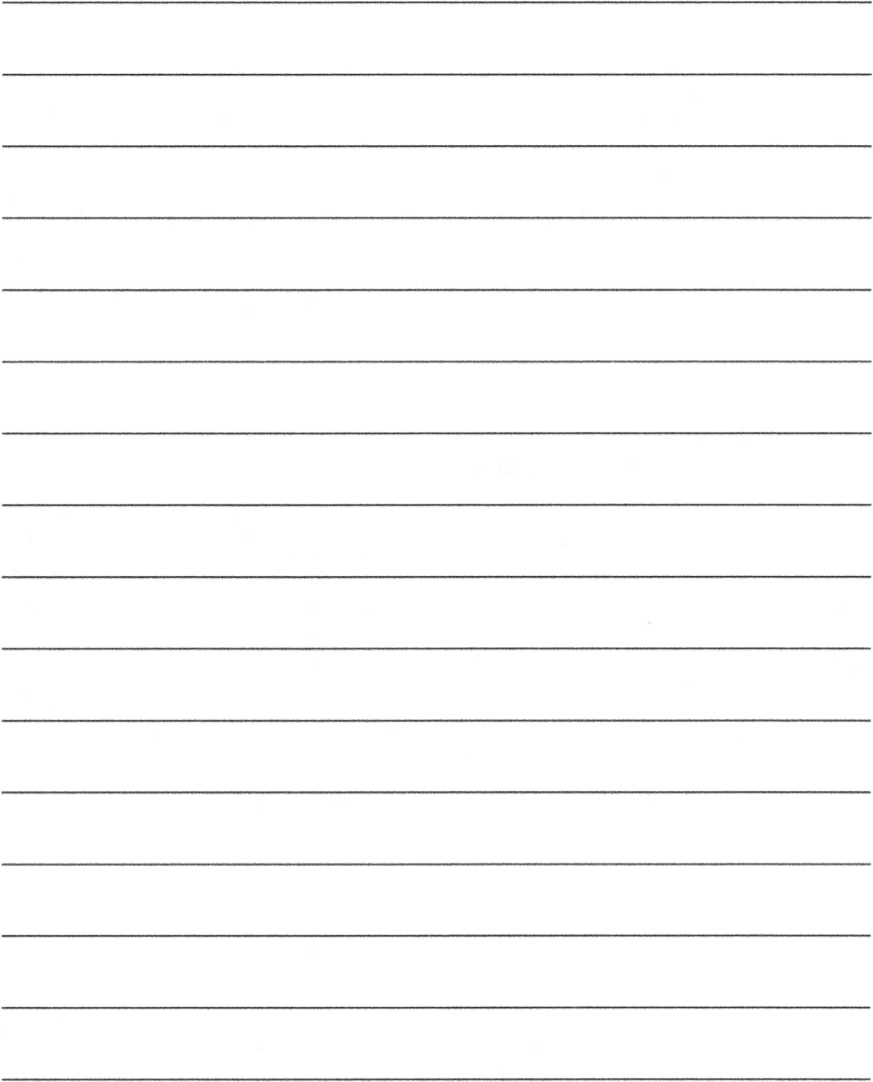

_____

_____

_____

_____

_____

_____

_____

_____

_____

_____

_____

_____

_____

_____

_____

_____

_____

_____

_____

_____

_____

_____

_____

h) early centuries CE to early second millennium CE: Earthen
   Urbanism under Canopy, Amazonia

Starter context: LIDAR reveals platforms, causeways, canals, and
planned settlements under forest cover, pointing toward agro-urban
mosaics that reframe what counts as a city in the tropics. Bring this
into your timeline to show that stone is not the only way to
monumentalize.

- Title:

  _____

- Date   range   and   location:

  _____

- Why it matters:

_____

_____

_____

_____

_____

- Mainstream reading you will test:

_____

- Alternative reading you will test:

_____

- Next action:

_____

- Sketch box, lidar-like plan with roads and platforms:
  [Space for drawing]

_____

_____

_____

_____

_____

_____

_____

_____

_____

_____

_____

_____

_____

_____

_____

_____

_____

_____

_____

_____

_____

_____

i) 1513 CE: Early Modern Portolan Maps that Should Not Exist

Starter context: your book notes early charts that appear to encode coastlines at odds with conventional capability claims. Use this as a historiography case, since maps are texts, not only pictures. What counts as solid cartographic evidence for the inheritance of older knowledge?

- Title:

  _____

- Date   range   and   location:

  _____

- Why it matters:

  _____

  _____

- Mainstream reading you will test:

  _____

- Alternative reading you will test:

  _____

- Next action:

  _____

- Sketch box, coastline, and grid comparison: [Space for drawing]

  _____

  _____

  _____

  _____

Your additional entries

Use these empty templates to capture more items as you read and research. Add as many copies of this page as you need.

Artifact or site:

_____

Date range and location:

_____

Why it matters:

_____

_____

Mainstream reading:

_____

Alternative reading:

_____

Next action:

_____

Sketch box:

_____

_____

_____

_____

Part B: Reflection Prompts

Which discovery most challenges your beliefs, and why

The goal here is not to win an argument; it is to become a better judge of claims. Pick one discovery at a time and walk it through these questions. Answer in whole sentences. If you change your mind midstream, strike through your original answer and write the revision below it. That is progress.

1) What surprised you first, the object itself or the implications

_____

_____

_____

_____

2) What is the strongest mainstream explanation, in your own words

(Avoid straw men, describe the best version you can find.)

_____

_____

_____

_____

3) What is the strongest heterodox reading, in your own words

_____

_____

_____

_____

4) List the three hardest facts that any explanation must fit

1. _____

2. _____

3. _____

5) What would change your mind

(Write a future test or piece of evidence that would push you the other way.)

_____

_____

_____

_____

6) What bias might be shaping your view

(Simplicity bias, preservation bias, silo bias, risk bias, comfort bias. Name it, then say how you will counter it.)

_____

_____

7) Write the most modest, defensible version of the claim you can support today

_____

_____

_____

_____

_____

_____

_____

_____

_____

_____

_____

Reflection templates for specific cases

Choose two or three of the following to develop fully.

Göbekli Tepe: coordination before cities

Anchor from the book: quarrying, transport, sockets, rebuilds, ritual burial, and a long planning horizon.

- My prior belief about pre-agricultural coordination was:

- What this site forces me to reconsider:

- If I could test one narrow hypothesis at the site, it would be:

- If confirmed, that would change my view by:

Antikythera Mechanism: precision in bronze

Anchor from the book: zodiac and calendar pointers, lunar anomaly correction, eclipse season spirals, and civic cycles.

- My prior belief about ancient computation was:

- What this device shows instead:

- One way I could build a paper or cardboard model to feel the ratios:

- What successful replication would teach me about ancient shop culture:

Archaeoacoustics: rooms that sing

Anchor from the book: measured peaks at 70 and 110 to 114 hertz, scale model data for Stonehenge, Chavín's instrument architecture duet.

- The most skeptical question I should ask is:

- The simplest field test I can run is:

- How I will record data and avoid overinterpreting:

Part C: Practical Exercises

Track celestial alignments and test ancient calendar systems

You will not need anything exotic. A stick, some string, a watch, a notebook, and patience will take you far. The idea is to turn cycles into things your hands and eyes can measure.

Exercise 1: Build a gnomon and find true cardinal directions

Purpose: measure the Sun's path to establish east-west and north-south, then mark a local meridian line on your ground or rooftop. This will anchor later alignment tests.

Materials:
A straight stick or dowel, at least 1 meter tall; a flat level area; small stones or chalk; a notebook and pencil; a watch or phone clock.

Steps:

1. Fix the stick upright on level ground.

2. Near local noon, mark the shortest shadow tip. Repeat the next day.

3. On a clear morning, starting two hours after sunrise, mark the shadow tip every ten minutes until two hours before sunset.

4. Draw a smooth arc through the marks.

5. Use a compass or geometric construction to find the east-west line by connecting equal-length shadow marks in the morning and afternoon; the perpendicular gives north-south.

6. Record the date and your latitude.

Record sheet:

Date: _____ Latitude: _____

Shortest shadow length: _____

Shadow marks log:

_____

_____

Sketch:

What this teaches: once you have a true local north-south line, you can test whether a structure or sightline favors a specific azimuth seasonally. Now you own a baseline that does not depend on a magnetic compass.

Link back to the book: a reliable gathering calendar needs reliable directions and seasonal markers, which is part of what coordinated projects like Göbekli Tepe imply.

Exercise 2: Track a 29.5-day lunar cycle

Purpose: build your own synodic month table and discover, by experience, why lunar solar calendars need intercalation.

Materials:
Notebook, pencil, small binoculars if available, clear horizon view.

Steps:

1. On day zero, record a new Moon when the thin crescent first becomes visible after sunset.

2. Each night, sketch the phase fraction and note the time the Moon rises or sets relative to the Sun.

3. When you return to the same phase under similar evening conditions, count the days elapsed.

4. Compare your count to the book's discussion of cycles that reconcile months and years.

Record table:

Date	Phase sketch	Time relation to the Sun	Notes

What this teaches: the month is not a neat fraction of the year, which motivates the 19-year cycle that brings lunar months and solar years back into step, a constant used by gear ratios in the Antikythera Mechanism.

Exercise 3: Paper dial, 19-year cycle

Purpose: make a working spiral dial on paper to feel how a long cycle advances.

Materials:
Two sheets of stiff paper; compass; ruler; pencil; scissors; brass fastener.

Steps:

1. On the first sheet, draw a flat spiral with three turns, divide it into 235 boxes to represent lunar months in 19 solar years.

2. On the second sheet, cut a small pointer window that slides along the spiral.

3. Mount the pointer on a rotating arm fixed at the spiral center.

4. Mark your current year on the outermost turn.

5. Advance one box per month and watch intercalary months appear where your calendar logic requires them.

6. Note how elegant it feels to track a long pattern with a compact spiral.

Sketch box and build marks:

What this teaches: with simple motion, you can keep a community calendar in step across decades, the same logic that the back dials of the Antikythera Mechanism embodied.

Exercise 4: Eclipse season awareness

Purpose: practice the idea of eclipse "seasons," not guaranteed events, and predict when a season is due using rules of thumb.

Materials:
Your 19-year spiral, a wall calendar, a notebook.

Steps:

1. Choose a known past eclipse date as an anchor.

2. Mark every six months plus about ten days thereafter as potential seasons, noting that visibility depends on location.

3. Over two years, watch whether eclipses cluster near your predicted windows.

4. Write what this felt like compared to reading a table.

Record sheet:
Anchor eclipse date: _____

Predicted seasons:

_____

Observed events, or lack thereof:

_____

What this teaches: the purpose of cycles is not perfect prophecy; it is coordination and preparedness. This is exactly how the book frames civic uses for astronomical cycles.

_____

Exercise 5: Horizon alignment check

Purpose: test a proposed alignment at a local site, vista, or even a city street grid, and see if it keys to a solstice or equinox sunrise or sunset.

Materials:
Your gnomon baseline from Exercise 1; a handheld compass for rough azimuth; a phone with an augmented reality sky app, if allowed; camera.

Steps:

1. Stand at the observation point and mark the sightline to a horizon notch or street canyon.

2. Use your local north-south line to estimate the azimuth.

3. Compare with known solar azimuths at solstices and equinoxes for your latitude.

4. Return on suspect dates and take photographs at the same time of day.

5. Record whether the match is within a degree or two, or whether it misses by much, and decide what that means for intent versus coincidence.

Record sheet:

Site: _____ Latitude: _____

Sightline azimuth estimate: _____

Dates tested: _____

Observations:

What this teaches: alignments can be loose or tight. Repeatability matters. You learn quickly why builders might have chosen visible, stable features on the horizon to carry memory across generations.

Exercise 6: Archaeoacoustics, safe and simple mapping

Purpose: map hot spots where a room "answers" a voice or tone, then compare to the book's highlighted frequencies.

Materials:
Tone generator app, small portable speaker, sound level app, measuring tape, chalk, or painter's tape.

Steps:

1. Pick a room you can safely test.

2. Sweep a tone from 60 to 300 hertz at low volume.

3. Walk a grid and mark where the sound blooms or dips.

4. Note any strong response near 70 or 110 to 114 hertz, then try a sustained hum there.

5. Sketch your pressure map.

6. Repeat with a second person to see if positions matter.

Record sheet:
Room dimensions: _____ Grid spacing: _____

Peak frequencies: _____

Map sketch:

What this teaches: you are learning to separate spectacle from physics, to catch the pattern your book emphasizes, rooms that select human-friendly bands and turn a single voice into a building-scale instrument.

Exercise 7: Logistics test, vibration, and friction

Purpose: evaluate whether rhythmic impacts reduce pull force on a sled over granular material.

Materials:

Small weighted sled; bags of sand; spring scale; two wooden slapper boards; metronome app.

Steps:

1. Prepare two parallel sand lanes, one dry, one lightly wetted.

2. Measure baseline pull force over 10 meters.

3. Repeat while two partners thump the boards at 2 hertz alongside the sled.

4. Log average force.

5. Graph the difference.

6. Write a short paragraph on whether this tells you anything useful about moving heavy blocks with teams and rhythm, without invoking levitation.

Data table:

Lane	Condition	Average pull force	Notes
1	Dry		
1	Dry, thump		

Lane	Condition	Average pull force	Notes
2	Wet		
2	Wet, thump		

What this teaches: vibration can change granular friction. You now have your own data to cite when the conversation moves from slogans to mechanisms.

Part D: Further Resources

Archives, documentaries, and research communities, plus a credibility checklist

Your book frames two hard truths: preservation bias hides coastal and canopy sites, and our own biases filter evidence that does not fit timelines. Use that to choose sources and peers without falling for noise.

1) Archives and open collections to mine

- **National and regional museum catalogs:** prioritize records with high-resolution images, measurements, and provenance notes.

- **Aerial and LIDAR portals:** look for raw terrain models and vegetation stripped visualizations where policy allows public access. You aim to inspect regularity across kilometers, not only a single hill.

- **University repositories:** theses and dissertations often contain site plans and measurements not published elsewhere.

- **Local survey reports:** small cultural resource assessments can hide major leads in tables and appendices.

Notes, target list:

_____

_____

2) Documentaries and lectures worth your time

You want presenters who show raw data, admit error bars, and demonstrate methods. Favor content that includes:

- side-by-side reconstructions and originals,

- cutaway diagrams,

- explicit dates with uncertainties,

- and clear statements of what would falsify the claim.

Your short list and why:

_____

_____

3) Research communities and field practice

- **Archaeoacoustics circles:** look for teams that publish impulse responses and frequency plots from field work, not only impressions.

- **Replication groups for ancient instruments and mechanisms:** makers who publish tooth counts, ratios, and build logs are gold for learning.

- **Landscape archaeology networks for canopy regions:** people comfortable with LIDAR and ground truthing will teach you how not to over-read pixels.

People or groups to follow, with one sentence on value:

_____

_____

4) Credibility checklist, use it every week

Paste this on your wall. Before you adopt a claim, test it against these six filters. Revise the list to suit your project.

1. **Mechanism:** Does the claim map to a testable mechanism you can replicate or at least simulate? If not, can it be reformulated so it does?

2. **Scale:** Is the effect plausible at the physical scale involved, not only in a lab demo?

3. **Context:** Does the material or site fit with known supply chains, training pipelines, and institutional needs of its era?

4. **Biases:** Which knowledge filters are at risk here, and how will you counter them?

5. **Redundancy:** could the knowledge have persisted through interruption via guilds, rites, or inscriptions? If yes, say how.

6. **Falsifiability:** what would change your mind, written in a single clear sentence. If you cannot write it, pause.

Your additions to the checklist:

_____

_____

_____

_____

_____

_____

Appendix: Clean Worksheets to Reprint

Use these blank pages for field days, museum visits, and lab nights. Copy and reuse.

Site visit sheet

Site name: _____ Date: _____

Weather and light:

_____

Coordinates or map ref: _____

Hypotheses you are testing today:

    1. _____

    2. _____

Sketch of plan and section:

Measurements:

Axis A B: _____

Axis C D: _____

Elevation changes: _____

Sightline azimuths: _____

Acoustics quick test:
Peak at 70 hertz: Yes / No
Peak at 110 to 114 hertz: Yes / No
Notes:

_____

Materials or workmanship notes:

_____

_____

Photographs taken, numbering scheme:

_____

Immediate interpretations, mainstream and alternative:
Mainstream:

_____

Alternative:

_____

Next actions:

_____

_____

Artifact analysis sheet

Object name:

_____

Material and size:

_____

Condition:

_____

Visible tool marks and tolerances:

_____

_____

Functional hypotheses:

_____

Comparanda from the book:

_____

_____

Sketch, orthographic views:

_____

_____

If this were part of a system, what else would exist:

_____

_____

What would falsify my preferred reading:

_____

_____

Mechanism worksheet, inspired by the Antikythera program

Cycle I want to model:

_____

Target ratio or tooth counts: _____

Pointer behavior desired: _____

Dial layout, circle or spiral: _____

Sketch gear train:

_____

_____

_____

_____

_____

_____

_____

_____

_____

_____

_____

_____

Test plan:

_____

_____

Notes as you debug, what bound, what cleared:

_____

_____

Takeaway about translating theory to craft:

_____

(Anchor idea: cycles stored as ratios in wheels, theory embodied. Keep your notes honest about where it jammed and why.)

Archaeoacoustics worksheet

Room or chamber:

_____

Volume estimate:

_____

Surface type: _____

Tone sweep results:

Peak frequencies: _____

Dead zones: _____

Subjective notes at 70 and 110 to 114 hertz:

_____

_____

_____

Map sketch with hot spots:

_____

_____

_____

_____

_____

_____

_____

_____

_____

_____

_____

Behavior with percussion versus voice:

_____

Interpretation: Does design or iterative selection seem likely here, and why?

_____

(Anchor idea: repeated selection for human-friendly bands points to intent without hype.)

Closing Guidance

- Keep your entries short at the start, then expand only where a test or replication is in reach.

- Do not argue with slogans; write what you actually measured or built.

- When you change your mind, record the moment and the reason. That is how a seeker becomes a reliable guide for others.

One line to carry forward:

Complexity is perishable, resilience is designed, memory must cross formats, and meaning is leveraged. Your workbook is one way to practice all four.

Extra Notes Pages

Use the rest of this section to draft, sketch, or paste clippings.

_____

_____

_____

_____

_____

_____

_____

End of Workbook

Conclusion

The oldest question in this book was never "did the ancients have engines," but "what did they understand well enough to make last—and what does that teach us about our own durability." By now you've heard the pattern in the stone and the bronze: knowledge rises, shatters, and rises again; fragments survive as workable clues; the future belongs to societies that can hear those clues without flinching. That is not mysticism. It's logistics, pedagogy, and patience wearing the mask of wonder.

We began with the "knowledge filter," with cultural amnesia and catastrophic forgetting—three forces that explain why anomalies are easy to dismiss and hard to absorb. They also explain why your task cannot end with fascination. If institutions defend timelines like fortress walls, then seekers must learn to bring measured evidence, not just louder claims. You've practiced that stance here: mainstream, where the data insists, heterodox where the data invites, humble throughout.

Consider the book's two emblematic witnesses. Göbekli Tepe shows coordination and surplus harnessed to meaning at a scale that predates the familiar city; the Antikythera Mechanism shows theory embodied so tightly in metal that one crank replays the heavens. They are separated by millennia and method, yet they whisper the same thing: people, given time and feedback, will build systems that exceed bare necessity—and those systems are perishable unless their scaffolds of training, patrons, and tools persist. Hold both insights as you judge our own systems.

Across chapters, a practical playbook emerged. First, honor the long apprenticeship: prototype, test, revise, and write the lessons where novices can actually find them. Second, expect acceleration once trustworthy coordination exists—and design governance that rewards stewards, not just founders. Third, mitigate recurrent vulnerabilities: coastal exposure, fragile supply lines, predation on provisioning, and knowledge locked to one language or sect. These are not slogans; they are maintenance instructions for civilizations.

From that playbook flows a simple ethic. Build legible systems. If a newcomer cannot run the plant from on-site labels and diagrams, you are courting amnesia. Audit dependencies, and shorten the list of things you cannot replace within a season. Celebrate the boring work in public: filters cleaned, manuals updated, apprentices trained. The ancients did not rely on genius alone; they endured on routine. So will we.

This ethic is already encoded in the material lessons you met along the way. Roman harbor concrete is not magic; it's a patient recipe that lets water finish the work. Damascus is not a legend; it's disciplined thermal choreography. The Delhi pillar is not stainless; it's a composition and process that grew its own shield in that particular air. Each case rebukes our love of instant performance and vindicates design for repair, for healing, for the long tail. Materials are memory; write wisely.

So what do the echoes finally say about the "big question"—are we the first? At the scale of fossil-fuel global industry, yes. At the scale that matters for survival—durable precision, long-horizon planning, resilient coordination—we have predecessors. They are not rivals; they are collaborators across time. If we learn from them, our future will look less like a fireworks show and more like a well-run workshop beside a well-tended watershed: modest in appetite, generous in copying, careful in caring for people we will never meet. That is how a civilization becomes hard to erase.

Your next steps are clear, and they are beautifully ordinary:

- Treat the past like a library, not a museum. Read it for methods you can reuse. Start with underwater shelves, with apprenticeship debris, with rituals as registries of counts and cycles.

- Preserve knowledge in triple form: a practiced craft, a durable analog, an open digital. Assume the rebooters will have sharp minds and dead batteries.

- Make your city legible to strangers. Inscribe the critical summaries into the buildings themselves; keep multiple copies, in multiple tongues, in multiple places. Reward the custodians.

If you carry only one sentence out of these pages, let it be this: complexity is perishable, but care scales. The pillars on the plateau and the gears in the sea are not merely proofs that "they could"; they are instructions for how we still can—how to bind meaning to maintenance, how to store memory in matter, how to leave good echoes behind. When your descendants listen to us, let them find more than fragments. Let them find diagrams that teach, workshops that welcome, watersheds that still run clear, and a sky map etched where night can read it. Then they will say what we have said of others: they thought ahead; they left us instructions; they made it easy to keep going.

FORBIDDEN HISTORY SERIES

Explore other books in the series

Hidden Truths

*The Untold Histories, Lost Civilizations, and Forbidden Secrets
They Never Wanted You to Discover*

Secret Codes

*Mystical Manuscripts, Undeciphered Languages, and the Messages
That Could Rewrite History*

Lost Knowledge

*Ancient Technologies, Hidden Sciences, and the Secrets of
Civilizations Before Time*

Banned Maps

*Ancient Charts, Ley Lines, and the Geographic Mysteries That
Redefine Our Past*

*Sacred Texts — Hidden Scriptures, Lost Gospels, and the Secrets
of the Bible They Don't Want You to Know.*

www.ingramcontent.com/pod-product-compliance
Lightning Source LLC
Chambersburg PA
CBHW060736050426
42449CB00008B/1250